WITHDRAWN

The Early Career of Malcolm Cowley

The Early Career
of Malcolm Cowley

A HUMANIST AMONG THE MODERNS

James Michael Kempf

1935 1985

LOUISIANA STATE UNIVERSITY PRESS

BATON ROUGE AND LONDON

Copyright © 1985 by Louisiana State University Press
Manufactured in the United States of America

Designer: Joanna Hill
Typeface: Linotron Garamond #3
Printer and binder: Edwards Brothers

LIBRARY OF CONGRESS CATALOGING IN PUBLICATION DATA

Kempf, James Michael.
   The early career of Malcolm Cowley.

   Bibliography: p.
   Includes index.
   1. Cowley, Malcolm, 1898–   . 2. Authors, American—
20th century—Biography. 3. Critics—United States—
Biography. I. Title.
PS3505.0956Z73   1985   811'.52   84-21290
ISBN 0-8071-1217-8

PS
3505
0956
Z73
1985

The author is grateful to Malcolm Cowley for permission to reprint portions
of his letters (Malcolm Cowley Papers, Newberry Library, Chicago), and for
permission to reprint excerpts from *Exile's Return: A Literary Odyssey of the
Nineteen Twenties* (New York: Viking Press, Inc., 1951), copyright © 1951 by
Malcolm Cowley; and from *And I Worked at the Writer's Trade* (New York: Viking
Press, Inc., 1978), copyright © 1978 by Malcolm Cowley.

Chapter Four previously appeared, in slightly different form, as "Encountering
the Avant-Garde: Malcolm Cowley in France, 1921–1922," in *Southern Review*,
XX (January, 1984), 12–28.

Publication of this book has been assisted by a grant from the Andrew W.
Mellon Foundation.

For Wallace W. Douglas and Willard Thorp

Contents

Preface

Malcolm Cowley, whose early years as a writer are the subject of
this study, attracted my interest for several reasons. His long and
active career spanned the history of American literature during
most of our century and thus provided me with an opportunity to
study that history intensively. His varied interests and ability to
function in many diverse fields, including professional writing,
editing, publishing, teaching, cultural organizations, and what
one might describe as the business of being a man of letters in the
modern world, all appealed to my sensibility. But the impulse
toward writing this study goes back to my undergraduate years.

My senior thesis was on F. Scott Fitzgerald. While working on
it I gained a fairly extensive acquaintance with the literary criticism of Fitzgerald's work. I was particularly impressed by the
essay Cowley had written on *The Crack-Up*. It made eminent
sense to me compared with much of my other reading because it
placed Fitzgerald's work in his time. Cowley had argued that the
force of this author's perspective was partly the result of personal
and social circumstances that gave him insight into the new mon-
eyed society of industrial America while he still retained a strong
memory of the stable midwestern society from which he came.
Fitzgerald's writings, Cowley said, thus provided both a sharp
picture of urbanized America and a penetrating criticism of the
transformation that society had undergone in his own era. At the
time I did not know how much Cowley's own experiences had
contributed to his sensitivity to both Fitzgerald and the social

changes of the 1920s, but I appreciated and was influenced by his writings.

Seven years later, after military service and a long immersion in graduate studies of English literature, I had an opportunity to renew my interest in the literary history of the 1920s. I was in a seminar that visited the Newberry Library to encourage our use of the treasures assembled there. After a discussion of Shakespeare first folios, illuminated manuscripts of the Middle Ages, western historical records, and the papers of Sherwood Anderson, the librarian mentioned that the Malcolm Cowley papers were a relatively new acquisition that strengthened the library's collection in the field of modern American literary history. My ears pricked up at Cowley's name. I inquired about his papers and learned that parts of the collection had been used by scholars but that nobody had so far studied it in its entirety.

Later I worked with the Cowley papers for two years without following to the end all the paths they opened. The collection included letters, drafts, and press clippings, some of them dating back to 1915. It was rich and varied, and it revealed more consistency of character and judgment than I had expected to find.

It also revealed Cowley to be a man stubbornly loyal to his chosen career, professional writing, and his fellow writers. His files contain cases of records concerning his work and support for various American cultural organizations. For fifty years he helped advise the Yaddo writers' colony in Saratoga Springs, New York. Cowley also served on the founding committees (and as the first judge) of the Bollingen Prize for Poetry (after it left Washington) and the National Book Awards. In the early 1950s he advised the Rockefeller Foundation on how to support literary magazines. He twice served as president of the National Institute of Arts and Letters, and he was chancellor of the American Academy of Arts and Letters for thirteen years. In both capacities he spent months creating and dispensing awards to both new and established writers. He also spent time over the years reading and editing manuscripts and advising writers and literary scholars in his roles as a director of Yaddo and as literary consultant to the Viking Press. His private papers revealed him as working quietly behind the scenes to bring to publication books by dozens of poets, novelists, and scholars, and writers on public affairs. The record of this accomplishment is almost unknown to the general public, but it parallels his impressive career as a working author.

Cowley's literary beliefs in mid-career were an outgrowth of the beliefs with which he started. I decided to limit myself to his early career because it foreshadowed everything that would follow. My story would be that of a young man—a country boy, by his own description—venturing into the seas of cosmopolitan literature. Buffeted by winds of doctrine, he was determined to follow the course laid down by his original perceptions. His intellectual adventures reveal some unexpected aspects of the battle for and against modernism in America.

Several people have helped me bring this book to publication. Lewis P. Simpson of Louisiana State University was responsible for stimulating the interest of Louisiana State University Press in the study. At LSU Press, Beverly Jarrett, the associate director and executive editor, Catherine F. Barton, the managing editor, and Shannon Sandifer, my supervising editor, patiently guided me through the publishing process. Trudie Calvert performed painstaking copy-editing chores and advised me on matters of documentation. I would also like to thank Diana Haskell, the curator of modern manuscripts at Chicago's Newberry Library, who assisted me with the library's Malcolm Cowley collection. The Board of Higher Education and Ministry of the United Methodist Church awarded me a Cokesbury fellowship, which provided needed funds during part of the research. I have profited from discussions with Diane Eisenberg, whose bibliography of Malcolm Cowley was an invaluable aid, and from talks with Hans Bak of the Katholieke Universiteit in Nijmegen, Holland, who is currently completing a study of Malcolm Cowley.

Many persons have given me advice and encouragement. I wish especially to thank the following: Moody E. Prior, Harrison

Hayford, Gerald Graff, James A. Grimshaw, Jr., Alfred Kern, Adolph and Maxine Kempf, and Harry and Ada Kinne. Ruth Nuzum of Boulder, Colorado, generously helped me with recent bibliographical information concerning Cowley. Dode Jones of Colorado Springs patiently typed various drafts of the manuscript. I have dedicated the book to two former teachers. Willard Thorp got me started in the business of literary scholarship. Without the help of Wallace Douglas this study would not have been completed. Finally, special thanks are due Malcolm Cowley, who read the manuscript, corrected several errors of chronology, and clarified the context of several incidents described in the text.

The Early Career of Malcolm Cowley

CHAPTER I

Some Critical Forerunners
of Modernism in America

Malcolm Cowley is often mentioned as among the critics who
defined European modernism for a new generation of American
writers and artists. Four other names that appear in this connection are those of José Ortega y Gasset, Alfred Barr, Edmund Wilson, and Kenneth Burke, but their ideas and influence have not
been sufficiently analyzed or explained. Some of them—Cowley
in particular—have suffered from misrepresentation or neglect.

In 1923 Ortega published an influential work, *The Modern
Theme*, describing the often severe dehumanization of human
forms in modern art. He was sympathetic to the aesthetic theories
governing the new art but noted that it was primarily distinguished by its thorough break from the tradition of western
European art that had prevailed for almost four centuries.[1]

A decade later, in 1936, Alfred Barr wrote the catalog for a
retrospective exhibition of European abstract art at the Museum
of Modern Art. In it he said that at least two motives characterized the diverse styles of modern artists. The first was a conscious,
and conscientious, repudiation of the tradition that had dominated European art since the Renaissance, that of mimetic, humanistic, and naturalistic painting and sculpture. Barr also
briefly noted another possible motive behind the new aesthetics,
one that was evident in such disparate movements as Fauvism,
Cubism, Simultanism-Orphism, Italian Futurism, German Ex-
pressionism, and Russian Constructivism and Suprematism. This

1. José Ortega y Gasset, *The Dehumanization of Art and Other Essays on Art,
Culture, and Literature* (Princeton, 1968).

motive was an apparent deep alienation among European artists from the social world of late nineteenth- and early twentieth-century Western industrial society, which no longer seemed a subject of aesthetic interest or pleasure for artists.[2]

Similarly, in *Axel's Castle* (1931) Edmund Wilson argued that the difficulty of comprehending the works of many modern writers represented a literary parallel to the aesthetics of the visual arts. Wilson declared that this phenomenon was the product of the ideas and intellectual and aesthetic undercurrents of nineteenth-century Romanticism, particularly as these were expressed in the French Symbolist movement in the arts. The Symbolist aesthetic, Wilson argued, was characterized by a preoccupation with private sensibility, nostalgia for archaic civilizations, a tendency toward withdrawal into fantasy, the materials of which could be transmuted into artistic form, and the notion that artists should remain aloof, or withdraw altogether, from contemporary life. The subject matter of modern art was often artistic works of the past, used to imply that art is free from historical or social conditions. Discussing T. S. Eliot's literary theories, Wilson used the term "Aestheticism" to name the spirit of modern art: its tendency to be wholly self-contained and self-referential. This theory, he said, explained the museumlike quality of, for example, James Joyce's *Ulysses* or Eliot's own *The Waste Land*.[3]

In his book *Counter-Statement*, also published in 1931, Kenneth Burke agreed with many of Wilson's insights about the nature of modern literature but took exception to his implication that a healthy literature should concern itself with social issues and not with psychological and moral problems. In his discussion of modern poetics and in his analysis of such modern European writers as Thomas Mann and André Gide, Burke urged that modern art was distinct not only from post-Renaissance western European art but from all Western art since that of the Greeks

2. Alfred H. Barr, Jr., *Cubism and Abstract Art* (1936; rpr. New York, 1974).
3. Edmund Wilson, *Axel's Castle* (1931; rpr. New York, 1969).

and Romans. Burke said that much modern literature emphasized the artist's unique, special, and often alienated sensibility. To understand modern literature, especially its "difficulty," Burke argued that it was necessary to understand the economic, political, social, and cultural environment that surrounded and conditioned it. Thus the French Symbolists' doctrine of art-for-art's-sake was a consequence of new cultural circumstances, in which art had become overwhelmed by an industrial and technological culture. The Symbolist artists had made a virtue of their lack of audience, in some cases aggressively defying public taste and social conventions. Their social alienation, Burke wrote, was sometimes rooted in personal psychology, as in Remy de Gourmont's feelings of social inadequacy.[4]

Almost all discussions of modern art since these early ones have borrowed the terms of their analysis: antitraditionalism, antinaturalism, social alienation and bohemianism, antirational and symbolist communication, and the dehumanization and abandonment of logical and objective narrative forms or visual perspective. The nihilism of modern art and the antisocial behavior of artists have often been attributed—as Kenneth Burke first noted—to the cultural climate of an industrial and commercial society in which artists no longer have a stable public audience to judge and appreciate their work and the spiritual values and sensitive emotional expression of art seem overwhelmed by material and practical concerns.

Each of these early critics was primarily concerned with the modern art of Europe. Malcolm Cowley is generally recognized as the first critic to describe the influence of modern aesthetics and cultural ideas on the work and lives of American artists of the first half of the twentieth century. His book *Exile's Return* was a historical memoir of his part in the journey of a generation of American artists to Europe in the 1920s after World War I, their encounter with the explosion of modern art, and their return when the monetary rate of exchange became less favorable.

4. Kenneth Burke, *Counter-Statement* (1931; rpr. Berkeley, 1968).

The book justifiably made Cowley's reputation. Along with his later critical work on writers such as William Faulkner and Ernest Hemingway, it made him a significant figure in American twentieth-century literary history.

Cowley's writings on American literary life during the 1920s and 1930s have been major sources for a number of literary, as well as social and political, analysts of our modern cultural history. Many of these critics, however, have tended to treat Cowley too briefly, discussing him only in connection with the larger movements of social, aesthetic, and political revolt characteristic of the Jazz Age and the Depression years. And they have often followed a fairly standard, though divided, line of interpretation. One view of Cowley is represented in an essay published in 1973 by Philip Young. Young argued that Cowley's greatest literary contribution was *Exile's Return*, in which he explained the literary ferment and social alienation of American writers during the 1920s, and his later seminal essays on the great modern American writers such as Hemingway and Faulkner. Young implied in his essay that Cowley's understanding of the early century avant-garde movement in American art was so astute because of his closeness to that historic cultural event.[5]

Another common view of Cowley and his work is given by Reed Whittemore, who argued sympathetically in 1978 that Cowley's work derives its particular virtue not from his participation in the American avant-garde but from the critical values he developed during his radical political enthusiasm of the 1930s and his adoption of Marxist ideas about the social value of art. Whittemore believes that this political radicalism led both to Cowley's ultimate repudiation of earlier avant-garde aesthetic and social values and to his brilliant analysis of those values. Thus Cowley's often stated insistence that art has social implications

5. Philip Young, "For Malcolm Cowley: Critic, Poet, 1898–," *Southern Review*, IX (Autumn, 1973), 778–95.

and that artists have social responsibilities has been the distinguishing mark of his writing at a time when such ideas are unfashionable and have been submerged by modern "formalist" theories of art.[6]

Cowley has not been immune to the hostilities of contemporary literary quarrels. In an essay on the so-called "postmodern" fiction of Americans such as John Barth, Thomas Pynchon, and Robert Coover, who have used the experimental stylistic and narrative techniques first developed by European writers such as Joyce, Marcel Proust, and Franz Kafka, Joseph Epstein wrote that the radical politics of Cowley, Kenneth Burke, Edmund Wilson, and others in the 1930s were only another form of anti-Americanism, which paralleled their avant-garde attacks on America in the 1920s. Those attacks, he said, continue in the "experimental" fiction of contemporary writers and in the radical politics of intellectuals in the 1960s and 1970s.[7]

The neo-Marxist Christopher Lasch, however, has repeatedly cited Cowley as a prime example of his thesis that the rebellious American intellectuals and artists of the 1920s and 1930s were insincere and confused in equating their cultural protest with political protest. According to Lasch, avant-garde intellectuals and writers of the early twentieth century were in fact disguised publicists for capitalism, constituting a new class of bourgeois intellectuals whose work helped shape the mass consumer society needed by capitalism to survive and who savored the rewards and comforts provided them by a grateful system.[8] As I hope to demonstrate in this study, none of these portrayals of Cowley is complete, accurate, or convincing.

6. Reed Whittemore, "Books Considered," *New Republic*, April 29, 1978, pp. 29−31.

7. Joseph Epstein, "A Conspiracy of Silence," *Harper's*, CCLV (November, 1977), 77−92.

8. Christopher Lasch, *The New Radicalism in America, 1889−1963* (New York, 1965), 71−72; and "Alienation à la Mode," *Nation*, July 5, 1980, pp. 21−22.

Yet older cultural critics, too, often carrying the scars of long-ago literary battles, have insisted that Cowley's politics, particularly during the 1930s, were wrongheaded and naive. Thus Cowley was described by Alfred Kazin in his 1965 memoir on the 1930s as one of the most influential writers of that era, one who finally, because of political anger, turned the book section of the *New Republic* into a "Stalinist organ" of propaganda.[9] The charge of Stalinism with regard to Cowley has been serious, part of the sometimes bitter conflicts of modern literary history, and needs clarification, though the scope of this study does not permit a detailed analysis of Cowley's political writing in the 1930s.

In contrast with Kazin, however, Henry Dan Piper writing in 1967 summarized his own study of Cowley's writing in the 1930s by stating that on close examination it represents an older tradition of Western art and liberal political thought, a humanism upholding the ideals of literary mimesis, rational discourse and conventions in art, and a voice for morality.[10]

That Cowley is seen almost as two different persons by scholars of differing persuasions, backgrounds, and critical methods is evident in another published essay on his work. Citing an essay on Van Wyck Brooks that Cowley wrote in 1936, which Joseph Epstein used as evidence of Cowley's anti-Americanism, Lewis P. Simpson wrote in 1976 that when looked at as a whole, Cowley's published work is more complex than has generally been noticed. While apparently preoccupied with a "poetics of exile," the alienated aesthetic and social ideas that have dominated Western intellectual and artistic life for almost two hundred years, Cowley has, in fact, taken for his subject the role of the writer in the modern world. And Cowley's major theme in this enterprise has been to show the public, as well as writers themselves, the ways in which artists must recognize and come to terms with their human need for social community, even though social revolt and

9. Alfred Kazin, *Starting out in the Thirties* (Boston, 1965), 15–20.
10. Henry Dan Piper, Introduction to Malcolm Cowley, *Think Back on Us: A Contemporary Chronicle of the 1930's* (Carbondale, 1967).

spiritual isolation have been the characteristic themes in modern art. Paradoxically, Simpson pointed out, the American literary tradition, which Cowley spent much of his career coming to terms with—and helping to define—was one of individual solitude, as indeed were Cowley's own life and work. For Simpson, then, Cowley's work could be said to deal with the central issue of a particular American tradition of literature.[11]

All these conflicting assessments of Malcolm Cowley reveal, I believe, not only that Cowley is an interesting figure in his own right in modern American literary history but also that a study of his life permits one to focus on issues that have remained subjects of critical conflict for much of modern cultural history. These issues include a debate over what modern American art represents, why political and social rebellion by American artists has been so persistent, and what constitutes "Americanism" with respect to American writers and the American literary tradition. That Cowley's involvement with modern art and Communist politics has been sometimes vigorously attacked by polemicists from both the political left and the right may say less about Cowley than about the confusions of American cultural politics. The persistent misunderstanding of his views is, however, puzzling.

A further example of this misunderstanding is the assertion that Malcolm Cowley's work in the 1930s resulted only from a flirtation with radical Communist politics. This assertion obscures the more complex reality of his intellectual development and his actual writing. Those who make it must ignore his persistent attempt in those years to clarify, counteract, and socialize the intellectual and aesthetic tradition of modern art, with which for almost a decade before 1930 he had been locked in personal struggle.

11. Lewis P. Simpson, "Malcolm Cowley and the American Writer," *Sewanee Review*, LXXXIV (Spring, 1976), 220–47; rpr. Simpson, *The Brazen Face of History* (Baton Rouge, 1980). The essay to which Simpson referred was Malcolm Cowley, review of Van Wyck Brooks's *The Flowering of New England*, *New Republic*, LXXXVIII (August 26, 1936), 79–80.

From this perspective, Cowley's opinions in the 1930s can be seen as having evolved from earlier intellectual convictions as much as from the radicalism he developed during the Depression and from the adoption among American and European intellectuals of Marxist methods of social analysis and argument. His major writings, in fact, were not written to support the "overthrow of American capitalism" or as a defense of "Stalinism." Rather, the "rehumanization" of twentieth-century society remained Cowley's major literary subject just as it had been in the 1920s. Cowley's support for American Communism was given with neither a whole heart nor a full ideological commitment but as a so-called fellow traveler, and it ended in the 1930s, when he perceived that Communist political practices and Marxist theory could be as dehumanizing as those of capitalism and fascism.

It is not an exaggeration to say that the one book which has done the most to influence subsequent critical interpretations of the complicated ways in which modern European art influenced American writers of the early century is Malcolm Cowley's *Exile's Return*. Even recent critics who have taken issue with Cowley's view of the 1920s have noted that it is Cowley's book against which other interpretations must be measured.[12]

Few critics, however, have seemed to understand Cowley's intentions in *Exile's Return*. Because it was published in 1934, literary historians have rightly assumed that the book was part of the general repudiation, then current in the American literary community, of the often antisocial attitude of artists that was an important cultural aspect of the 1920s. Disturbed by the political crisis of the Depression, the literary community was turning to social commitment and abandoning a "modern" art of private sensibility; and *Exile's Return* was one testament to a changed intellectual and artistic atmosphere.[13]

12. Geoffrey Wolff, *Black Sun: The Brief Transit and Violent Eclipse of Harry Crosby* (New York, 1976).

13. Robert E. Spiller, *The Cycle of American Literature* (New York, 1956), 187.

But Cowley's book was more than just a memoir of repudiation or a political polemic. It has remained influential because it was essentially a work of literary history, a book whose purpose was to explain and criticize a social and cultural environment. Cowley's theme was that historical conditions deeply influenced art and artists. He argued that to understand American cultural modernism in the 1920s one had to understand how American artists had absorbed, in varying degrees, the social, political, and aesthetic doctrines first developed in nineteenth-century France by Symbolist artists and then transmitted across the Atlantic. Cowley traced this influence, as well as that of the cultural criticism in the 1920s of older writers such as H. L. Mencken and Van Wyck Brooks, which, he said, had reinforced the alienated temperament of younger artists, although their experiences before and after World War I had been part of a great upheaval and transformation of American society itself.

It is surprising that a book so lucid and eloquent in its thesis has remained so controversial and its author somewhat misunderstood. For Cowley's theme in *Exile's Return* and the ethos it represented were traditional and old-fashioned. From the perspective of modern times, it was a voice which in morals and ethics represented a "conserving" defense of a tradition of liberal humanism and in art a defense of the principles of rational, mimetic, and naturalistic style and techniques.

Part of the misunderstanding of Cowley's career may be his own fault. In *Exile's Return*, for example, Cowley contributed to the confusion about his motives and ideas by his satirical description of his own behavior and of his relationship to the avant-garde artists of Paris and New York with whom he associated in the early 1920s. In his history of the literary life in those years he unfortunately gave his own responses and judgments in somewhat condensed form, presumably because he wanted to stay in the background while portraying the complexity of the era. Sometimes he failed to make it clear that he was speaking ironically. One example is a section called "The Greenwich Village Idea" in which he listed eight notions widely held by the villagers. Some readers took the list as a serious statement of his own ideas at the time, whereas they were ideas he had always regarded as faintly ridiculous.

Honest as he was in portraying his personal history, his account of his attitudes and developing responses to the culture that was exploding around him was occasionally misleading. The history presented in his book was one of gradual evolution. He told of how his writer friends had begun their careers as essentially naive and enthusiastic young men bred in middle-class security before World War I. The theme of alienation, which has been so prominent in modern literature, was a result, Cowley's book implied, of a world in upheaval.

The influence of modern art and modern culture on twentieth-century artists and intellectuals has been complicated and sometimes confusing. What we know about the history and implications of cultural modernism owes much to several early writers who did not have the benefit of a coherent theory to explain a by no means coherent subject. How Malcolm Cowley came to understand the major cultural movement of our century is the subject of the remainder of this study.

CHAPTER 2

The Education of a Poet, 1915–1920

Malcolm Cowley was first exposed to the new aesthetic ideas and practices of modern art during his years at Harvard. His letters and poems of that time reflect a young man largely absorbed with literature and his hometown friends.

It is notable that during his first two years in college, from the fall of 1915 to the spring of 1917, Cowley expressed his literary energies almost wholly in writing poems. Of sixteen he published during his first year and a half of college, some were autobiographical; most of the others reflected an imitative awareness of the modern experimental aesthetic. But Cowley nowhere revealed any understanding of the theoretical ideas behind modern styles. Indeed, it is apparent that like many young poets he absorbed stylistic influences well before thinking through or seeking to understand the implications of those styles. One early poem, titled "To a Girl I Dislike," illustrated a satiric bent of his personality. Apparently based on an evening with an uncompliant young woman, the poem undercuts the carefully built-up romantic emotion of the early lines with verbal revenge for the unrequited affection of the speaker:

Ever since I was a very little boy,
I have known a path that wound away through
            the birches and hemlocks;
And I remember.
How I always feared to follow it,
And liked to dream instead what lay at its
            end—

An Indian burying-ground, perhaps;
Or a cave of robbers, stored with fabulous
        riches;
Or a rotting cabin that had nursed some
        great hero.
And one day I followed the path,
Walking slowly out of fearfulness;
Starting back when I roused a covey of
        quail
From the maple scrub around the spring;
Only to find at the end of it,
Among the hemlocks and mossed birches,
A pigsty—
Like a piece of yellow glass set in
        filigreed platinum,
Or like your heart
Beneath the mysterious immobility of your
        beauty.[1]

In other poems from those early college years, Cowley seems
more aware of the subjects and styles of modern verse. One poem
called "Ragtime" attempted to capture the rhythms of popular
music. In another, titled "A Theme with Variations," Cowley
seems to have wanted to imitate or satirize a variety of contemporary New York poets and their styles. The first section is called
"As Written by Miss Edna St. Vincent Millay on Her Typewriter." The poem is a lament for the oppression of spirit a sensitive poet felt in urban New York:

My thoughts had festered in the heat
Three months; I could not do a thing.
The pavement boiled beneath my feet
Three months; I could not even sing
And wondered what the fall would bring.

1. Donald Hall (ed.), *Harvard Advocate Anthology* (New York, 1950),
151–52.

But yesterday at dusk, the lost
North wind sprang up after a rain,
And when I woke, I saw the frost
Had patterned lacework on the pane
And on my lips were songs again.

In the third section of the poem, titled "With Apologies to William Carlos Williams," Cowley satirized free-verse styles and imagism:

I wish I could pass out
lie with my toes towards the daisies
it must be cool even now
down there.
        Next autumn
there'll be wind, frost,
biting rain.
        I'll be peppy.
August is like last night's
Stale Pilsener.

The second section of the poem is a nonsatiric description of the summer heat of New York and the feverish thoughts and actions of a modern urban dweller. The last section is a prose poem describing Hindu imagery of Paradise seen behind a modern city of asphalt, a vision transformed by a special new consciousness. Fifty years later Jonathan Culler included the poem in the *Harvard Advocate Centennial Anthology* as one of the first examples of modern poetic styles published in the magazine.[2]

Cowley's early Harvard years were also characterized by close friendship with several hometown people who shared his interest in art and by affection for his family and rural home. In numerous letters written during 1915 and 1916 to Kenneth Burke, his closest hometown friend, Cowley revealed his deep feelings for

2. Jonathan D. Culler (ed.), *Harvard Advocate Centennial Anthology* (Cambridge, Mass., 1966), 109.

family and friends back in Pittsburgh. He especially recalled the family farm near the village of Belsano seventy miles from Pittsburgh, where he and his mother spent long summers, with his father joining them for weekends. The almost idyllic environment that Cowley presents in his letters mirrors the older America described by F. Scott Fitzgerald in *The Great Gatsby*. In the first volume of *Our Times*, Mark Sullivan described it as a nation still basically rural and agricultural, with small businesses dominating the economy. Life was slow, and people knew all their neighbors and their family histories. The singular fact of his boyhood is that, on the basis of available evidence, Cowley demonstrated no alienation whatsoever from his middle-class family environment. Unlike Ernest Hemingway, who later attacked the philistine attitude of Oak Park, or e. e. cummings, who wrote sardonic poems about "Cambridge ladies," or Hart Crane, who repudiated a Cleveland candy fortune, Cowley retained a lasting affection for the Pennsylvania countryside, with its quiet rolling hills and farm fields scattered among woods. And he appears to have greatly liked the people of his home community.[3]

Despite his attachment to home and family, Boston's and Harvard's intellectual riches stimulated him in ways that Pittsburgh could not. Indeed, the life of literature and his friendships with other student writers and graduate poets became a dominant concern of his early college years.

His academic courses were largely on the literary and philological subjects that constituted the basic liberal-arts curriculum in eastern colleges of the time. Cowley studied not only En-

---

3. Letters to Burke are in Malcolm Cowley Papers, Newberry Library, Chicago; subsequent references to letters are to correspondence contained in this collection, which Cowley generously gave me permission to use. Mark Sullivan, *Our Times* (New York, 1971), I. Cowley dedicated his first volume of poetry, *Blue Juniata* (New York, 1929), containing his work from 1919 through 1929, to his parents. For Cowley's boyhood in Belsano and Pittsburgh, the best source is a memoir, "Mother and Son," *American Heritage*, XXXIV (February–March, 1983), 28–35.

glish literature but German and French language and literature (though he had abandoned Latin after high school). Several of his letters suggest that Cowley was not greatly impressed or influenced by any of his Harvard teachers, except perhaps for two. Writing to Kenneth Burke in 1917, he noted that a high school teacher back in Pittsburgh was as stimulating as any he had his freshman year. But two of his Harvard professors did affect Cowley. One of his early poems and a book review he wrote in 1920 reflected his interest in English Romantic poetry acquired in a course he took from John Livingston Lowes.[4] After leaving Harvard, Cowley remained friendly with Lowes, who recommended him for an American Field Service Fellowship in 1921 and thus helped him to spend two years in France.

The other teacher who influenced him was a legendary figure to scores of Harvard students. Charles Townsend Copeland was an 1882 graduate, who, while a Harvard student, had campaigned to make English literature a fundamental part of the undergraduate education. In a letter of March 21, 1917, Cowley noted that "Copey's" course (which was famous for its rigorous writing requirements and Copeland's penchant for reading to his class long passages of literature) came close to being a prerequisite for student writers: "Copey is almost a parent of present day American literature. Our writing today is done by Harvard men, and Harvard men of prominence in literature always take Copey's course." Copeland served as Cowley's friend as well as instructor. When Cowley left Harvard to begin a writing career in New York in the winter of 1920, a brief letter containing ten dollars for train fare to New York was delivered. It was from Copeland.[5]

4. Interview with Malcolm Cowley by the author, July, 1975; Cowley to Burke, n.d., 1917. The poem "On Rereading Wordsworth" was published June 5, 1916, in the *Harvard Advocate* after Cowley had taken a course from Lowes. Several book reviews he wrote in 1921 reflected his study of English Romantic poetry in college, notably "The Chinless Age," *Dial*, LXX (January, 1921), 73–76.

5. Charles Townsend Copeland, "The Study of English Literature," in Hall

By the spring of 1917, his sophomore year, Cowley had published often enough in the *Advocate* to be elected to the staff.[6] The election, based mostly on his contributions of poetry and a few book reviews, indicated his acceptance as a full participant in the literary activity on which he had spent most of his extracurricular time. In a letter of March 31, 1917, to Kenneth Burke, he noted that his recent literary success made him for the first time feel like a legitimate poet and that the *Advocate* board and staff meetings provided the opportunity to discuss literature and expand his literary friendships, both of which he found rewarding and enjoyable.

Through his work on the *Advocate* Cowley met several Harvard graduate students who were active in Boston literary life. His friendship with one of these students in particular, S. Foster Damon, who had graduated in 1914, appears to have significantly influenced him. In a reminiscence written in the 1960s, Cowley remembered that in the spring of 1917 Damon had introduced him to a number of then largely unknown modern European writers and to such little-understood earlier writers as William Blake, Edgar Allan Poe, and Herman Melville. Damon's adventurous reading and enthusiasm for the Symbolist tradition of modern French literature and for writers such as Stéphane Mallarmé and Joris Karl Huysmans encouraged Cowley to read and study those writers during the next few years. Damon also took Cowley to regular meetings of the New England Poetry Society and to meetings of the newly formed Harvard Poetry Society. At a meeting of the former group he first met Amy Lowell, then the leader of the Boston free-verse movement. His reactions to the meeting show again his satirical view of life in these early years:

(ed.), *Harvard Advocate Anthology*, 44–46; Cowley to Burke, March 31, 1917; Malcolm Cowley, *And I Worked at the Writer's Trade* (New York, 1978), 55.

6. Cowley to Burke, March 21, 1917.

The New England Poetry Society is composed of Amy Lowell and her enemies. Chief of the opposite faction is probably Mrs. Marks (Josephine Preston Peabody). Formerly Amy was supported by [John Gould] Fletcher. And my Lord, those women were ugly: Amy stood with her back to the fire puffing away at a Fatima and looking very much like a volcanic mountain in eruption. . . . She advised me to smoke Alfred Dunhill pipes. She had found, she said, that the vulcanized bits didn't bite through. . . . I like Amy, and because I like her I am beginning to like her poetry. Besides her, there was an interminable boor, a man who wrote poetry about Calamity, five horribly ugly hags, and Amy's shadow. . . . Over in the corner, [Amy] the mountain queen would be haranguing a half dozen subjects and enemies.[7]

Damon also introduced Cowley to older Harvard writers such as Robert Hillyer, a prolific poet of the time who has been largely unread by later generations. From these men Cowley seems to have learned about the English "decadent school" of artists whose lives and art were a subject of interest and imitation among several of the literary men at Harvard.[8]

Cowley's literary interests during his early college years were interrupted in late March and early April of 1917 by America's entry into World War I. Harvard and numerous other colleges hurried to set up training facilities for volunteer military organizations. Cowley enlisted in the Harvard Regiment late in March. He also took an examination for the American Field Service Volunteer Corps, a noncombat medical organization, which many of his friends had joined before American entry into the war.[9] This action confirmed his tendency to follow the lead of older friends. The ambulance corps required little training, and so by May 11, 1917, he was writing from the American Field Service Paris

7. Cowley, *And I Worked at the Writer's Trade*, 35–50; Cowley to Burke, March 15, 1917, December 14, 1916.

8. Malcolm Cowley, *Exile's Return: A Literary Odyssey of the Nineteen Twenties* (New York, 1951), 35; Cowley to Burke, March 15, 1917.

9. Cowley to Burke, March 31, 1917; *ibid.*, n.d., 1917 file.

headquarters en route to the western front. Several poems published in the *Advocate* in late March, April, and early May reflected his changed awareness. Three of these were called "The Adventurer," "The Veteran," and "Ballade of French Service."

Cowley's first letters from France, in June, 1917, complained about the incompetence of the French officers commanding the military units and of the apparent chaos of the war organization. In a letter of June 7 he noted the exhaustion of the French fighting troops and commented that the men were tired of fighting. By the end of the month he had completed a tour of the Aisne front, which provoked an observation that what he had seen of France contradicted what he had been taught in college about the superiority of Europe's culture to America's. Yet he could respect the common soldiers he met. This observation increased his nationalist pride: "The chief thing I can see is that America is the best country in the world. France, Germany, and England are simply busy cutting each other's throats. The fabled universal education and culture of France is fabled. What is not a mean fable is their [the soldiers'] courage and endurance." [10]

Much of his time in June and July, 1917, was spent waiting for assignments, watching the war from a distance, and reading. In a letter of June 26 he described a German counterattack and confessed that he was "the poorest camion driver in the camp." The letter also listed the literature he had found time to read, including an anthology of French poetry of the years 1866–1888 containing poems by Baudelaire, Verlaine, and Rimbaud. He was, he wrote, impressed by how many of the poems were good. He had also been reading Dostoevsky and Arnold Bennett. He thanked Kenneth Burke for keeping him informed of the literary scene in New York by sending issues of the *Seven Arts*, the *Little Review*, and *Poetry* magazines.

In early July, 1917, he sent Burke a longer analysis of the effect the war was having on the men in the trenches and its polit-

10. *Ibid.*, June 1, 20, 1917.

ical implications for a postwar society: "For all we Americans re-
alize too little that at the end of the war every nation—yes, even
the United States—will be too exhausted in men and money, too
much in need of quick recuperation to go on with the old, happy-
go-lucky state of affairs. We Americans are fighting for personal
liberty, and yet after the fighting is over out of sheer need of effi-
ciency, we shall have to forego it." He added that his experience in France had confirmed his perception that a great historic
change was occurring because the war "was destroying the old
order of things" in Europe and only firsthand experience would
help one understand the full nature of the cataclysm. This letter,
which reveals Cowley's first detailed, though unsystematic, expression of political ideas, closed by noting that the war had to be
won to check German militarism: "And if the Germans win—oh
gawd. In the captured portions of France, they are making even
the little children work in the fields from five in the morning
until seven at night. Imagine a regime like that for the world." [11]

Cowley had gotten himself transferred from the ambulance
corps to the military transport service, in which he was now the
assistant driver of a five-ton Pierce Arrow truck, called a camion.
In September his unit drove to within twenty-seven hundred
yards of the trenches, close enough to see the wounded and shell-
shocked men but far enough away to provide a feeling of detach-
ment. He had also gone on leave to Paris, where the war seemed a
world away. A curious and unanticipated aspect of this double
existence provided Cowley with a perspective that he later called,
with some personal guilt and shame, a "spectatorial" attitude.
His letters over the months of July, August, and September,
1917, revealed the reason. While thousands were dying and
European civilization seemed to be crumbling, Cowley toured
Paris to inform Kenneth Burke back home of the cultural state of
France. A letter of July 12, for example, urged Burke to join the
ambulance service because, although living conditions were un-

11. *Ibid.*, July 4, 1917.

comfortable with cold nights and hot days, the ambulance drivers had "lots of free time to write verse." And he noted that the combat he saw only reinforced a dream he had, which, if fulfilled, would put him far from war. The dream was to "be a farmer and plow 100 acres and write verse." This goal he called his "ideal domestic life," to be completed by living with a woman companion with whom he could sit drinking cider. Such a life, he believed, would provide a welcome respite from the western front.

In late July, 1917, just before leaving for a week in Paris, where he intended to drink beer and buy a three-volume anthology of contemporary French poetry, he noted that as a camion driver he saw no dead men, only wounded ones, and that he was struck by the "pictorial effect of the war" when seen from behind the lines. The spectacle included shellbursts in the sky, searchlights making patterns, and occasional German bomb raids. While watching this war activity Cowley was making plans to translate French war stories, which he could sell in America because they were not copyrighted. In Paris he was fascinated by the legendary Left Bank artistic colony. He described to Burke the Café de la Paix, the army of prostitutes in Montmartre, and secondhand bookstalls along the Seine. [12]

This cultural voyeurism and seeming insensitivity to the slaughter reflected only one side of Cowley's personality. Along with his aestheticism, a vague social conscience struggled for expression. For example, in a letter to Burke of July 24 describing the "pictorial" scene of the war, he suddenly complained of the "chaos and insanity of the war" and how utterly stupid it seemed. A week later he indicated a premonition of the way the war would affect the generation of men who experienced it firsthand: "Service on the Western Front is the great common experience of the young manhood of today, an experience that will mould the thoughts of the next generation, and without which

12. *Ibid.*, July 24, 4, 1917.

one will be somewhat of a stranger to the world of the present and the future." [13]

Several letters written in September also revealed Cowley's awareness of the human casualties of the war environment. In one, he told of a young Princeton graduate in the camion service named Tat Brown A. Goortie, who had been harassed by other men in the camp to the point of attempted suicide. Cowley was troubled by the incident because the young man appeared intelligent and decent. But the trench warfare had created a humanly destructive atmosphere, which caused the men to take out their frustration on A. Goortie, apparently because he was a nephew of J. P. Morgan. [14]

By September, 1917, the destructive atmosphere of the camp was also affecting Cowley. He lamented the hours he and others wasted in interminable sessions of black jack ("the camp is a gambling hell") and vapid conversation. He noted the demoralization of many soldiers, including himself. He was also becoming aware that his literary interests differentiated him from the other men:

I have really decided that I am an out—I mean an intellectual by nature. All of which makes the last two years a blank for I certainly had need of finding out just what the companionship of his fellows—social, not intellectual—means to the artist. It means a constant struggle with his own nature; a constant repression of his impulses; and an acceptance of standards which while true to others are false to him! The mere discovery of this fact cannot annihilate instantly the desire to stand well with my fellows. . . . All this has a retroactive effect on the social desires. . . . Behold me in a few years a hermit like yourself." [15]

The problem Cowley was vaguely touching on in this letter to Kenneth Burke was one that would trouble him for many years. It concerned the need of modern artists to withdraw from social

13. *Ibid.*, July 31, 1917.
14. *Ibid.*, September 2, 1917.
15. *Ibid.*, September 11, August 20, 1917.

life in order to be true to their own standards. The social impulse to belong remained strong in Cowley all his life, but he also recognized that literary activity required solitude.

His poetic activity remained alive even in the military camps of France, though he was no aesthete. In early September he managed to publish a few poems in a French war-front publication and in the American Field Service bulletin. Unlike the average soldier, Cowley was feeding his intellect when possible. France provided the time and location to read the books his older Harvard companions had recommended. In a letter of September 11, 1917, he described his reaction to *The Picture of Dorian Gray* and Huysmans' *A Rebours*. Cowley's response to these so-called decadent writers of the 1890s was opposite to what might have been expected of a young avant-garde writer of the early twentieth century. Instead of adopting their ideas, he reacted with a surprisingly moral indignation. He wrote Kenneth Burke that he viscerally disliked the books:

A Rebours is Wilde exposed. Huysmans is terrible in his hates and disgusts. Authors he hates he gives to his servants for toilet paper. He likes childish things, however, the pictures of Gustave Moreau, Poe, Baudelaire, trite English expressions because they are English. He demonstrates the banality of the whole decadent movement. There is some difference between him and the youth who smoke Fatimas instead of Camels because they are "distinctively individual," but not much. He is the sort of person who would have one wife in Turkey and eight in Massachusetts, who would read Arsène Lupin in the original French, if he is English, and Victor Hugo and Dumas, he is in short an ass.[16]

Although Cowley did not as yet see decadent art as part of a larger tradition of avant-garde art, he did state, in a long letter to Burke written July 31, 1917, that the French Symbolist poets of the 1880s and 1890s had clearly served as a model for twentieth-century American free verse. He also noted that Amy Lowell's

16. *Ibid.*, September 11, 1917.

doctrines expounded in Boston in 1916, particularly a lecture titled "Vers Libre," were stolen from an essay Gustave Kahn had written in 1897, which Cowley read in France: "French avant-garde innovations show up in America 20 years later, from Baudelaire to Mallarmé." In a paragraph that defended American culture, he expressed his admiration for the Symbolists' achievement:

I thought of writing you once that France as an average is no more intellectual than the United States. "La Revue de Deux Mondes" costs three francs [then a high price], and is not on sale everywhere. The other magazines are often childish. . . . But on the other hand, a little reading of French poetry reveals a difference. Just as a matter of statistics, the Librairie Delagrave compiled an anthology of poetry from 1866 to 1914. None of the contents were bad; some of course were unsurpassed in English. The collection amounted to 2200 pages of fine print. As I said, just as a matter of statistics, could that be duplicated in England or America or in both? [17]

This letter is the first evidence that he was making tenuous connections between the avant-garde writers of nineteenth-century France and twentieth-century modern literary movements, although as yet he did not indicate what qualities connected the different movements.

In late September and October of 1917 Cowley found himself near the Aisne valley at the time a large, delayed French offensive began. The fighting on the Chemin des Dames gave Cowley his most lasting impression of the pure savagery of the war and its embittering effect on men caught up in it. He had recently seen and been disturbed by the effects of German gas warfare. Cowley also noted that the horror of the slaughter was dissuading many American volunteers from enlisting for combat service. He complained of French officers ceremonially decorating themselves for valor. The destructive psychological atmosphere, he wrote, con-

17. *Ibid.*, July 31, 1917.

tinued to demoralize the men and himself: "You can't imagine with what a feeling of absolute negation I play cards. . . . But I have climbed a little out of the depths."[18]

Part of his psychological improvement perhaps resulted from some romantic dreaming and a release of anger. In a letter of October 13, for example, he mentioned being haunted by "the dream of sitting by a fire in Cambridge" and being back in college, where he could feed his intellect. A week later he angrily denounced American officers for their treatment of enlisted men: "Once they are enlisted they are no longer people." He expected the letter to be censored, he wrote, because that invasion of privacy had become routine.[19]

By the end of October he was back in Paris staying at the University Union while waiting to return to Pittsburgh. His six-month service commitment was fulfilled, and he had decided that he wanted to go back to college.[20] He had witnessed the Aisne offensive, which had finally interrupted his almost month-long wait at the front. The battle had reinforced his desire to escape the war. In a poem he wrote at the time, imaginatively describing a soldier killed at the battle of Vimy Ridge, Cowley expressed the awareness, now conventional, that the innocence and enthusiasm with which many men had early marched off to war had ended only in bitter confusion and despair. Cowley also expressed some embarrassment with himself in the role of aesthetic tourist that he seems to have seen himself playing. "To a Dilettante Killed at Vimy" read as follows:

Years of small sorrows and of small
          endeavor;
Years of great plans, and mental cowardice;
And we that hoped they would not last
          forever:—

18. *Ibid.*, September 23, October 3, 9, 1917.
19. *Ibid.*, October 19, 1917.
20. *Ibid.*, October 29, 1917.

That's all. To cut the whole thing short,
      came this.
And yet the petty muddle you made of it;
The pose; the brave dreams foundered in
      a sea
Of idle talk, now seem to us resolved
Into clean metal by catastrophe.[21]

    Cowley returned to Pittsburgh in early December. He spent
most of December and January there, turning his experiences in
France into an article for the Pittsburgh *Gazette Times* about a
hometown boy back from an eyewitness view of history. The
article was his first piece of paid writing; he received a check for
three dollars. But America was now rapidly shipping equipment
and men to Europe, and Cowley could not ignore the war; he had
to prepare for real military service. By mid-December he had
taken an examination for the officer corps that flew balloons for
intelligence. His motive for joining this particular service was
not altogether patriotic or adventurous. He had learned in France
that the enforced subservience, trivial duties, and mass living
conditions of enlisted men are suffocating to intellectuals. Yet he
was not a leader either, Cowley believed, and in the balloon corps
he would be able to avoid commanding other men.[22]
    Before leaving for New York in January of 1918 to spend some
weeks in Greenwich Village with his Pittsburgh friends James
Light and Susan Jenkins and to visit Kenneth Burke at Columbia
University, Cowley learned that he had failed the aviation corps
physical examination because of a minor eye-muscle problem.
Cowley was angry and dispirited over being rejected for a virtual

    21. *Harvard Advocate*, February, 1918; rpr. Culler (ed.), *Harvard Advocate
Centennial Anthology*, 113.
    22. "U.S. Volunteer Tells of French Battle Front Visit—No Union Hours,"
Pittsburgh *Gazette Times*, January 6, 1918, sec. 5, p. 3; Cowley to Burke,
December 7, 14, 1917.

technicality.[23] This setback, however, provided the occasion for his literary friends to reinforce his aesthetic absorption.

In New York Cowley learned that Burke had deliberately failed some midyear examinations at Columbia because he had been absorbed in reading the novels and letters of Gustave Flaubert. The theme of failure became a source of satire for Cowley. During his time in Pittsburgh he had reviewed his poetry and had written Burke before going to New York that he now believed most of it was bad. He jokingly stated that "an heroic death" would be "indispensable," if it were ever to find a large audience. In a letter of January 17, 1918, Cowley again joked about the failures typical of the modern artist and Burke's examination failures. Their solace, he wrote, would be to "live in a garret and die for art."[24] This joking awareness of the often unknown and little-appreciated social position of artists in the modern world is another instance in his writing of a theme he would later develop in much of his later work, both in *Exile's Return* and in book reviews. His experience at Harvard the next year also gave him a deeper understanding of how serious his literary friends were about devoting their lives to art.

Cowley returned to Harvard in February of 1918 and enrolled in classes while he waited to begin military service. Almost immediately he sought out an older Harvard poet, Conrad Aiken, who had graduated in 1911. Cowley wanted to meet Aiken after reading a Boston publisher's edition of Aiken's long poem *The Jig of Forslin*, which impressed him deeply. At a series of meetings in late February, Cowley and Aiken began what developed into a lifelong friendship. Though Aiken was nine years older and had already published four volumes of poems, he responded warmly to Cowley's admiration. In a long essay Cowley wrote about Aiken more than fifty years after their first meeting, he

23. Cowley to Burke, December 14, 1917.
24. *Ibid.*, December 14, 1917, January 17, 1918.

remembered: "We both liked Boston in decay, we had notions about the French Symbolists, we spoke of achieving architectural and musical effects in verse (such as Aiken in fact had achieved) and we were fascinated by the political maneuvers of the poetry world without wishing to take part in them."[25]

Cowley's letters written at the time of his first meetings with Aiken confirm his recollections. In several written in late February, he described those meetings. Aiken told Cowley of his years in London and his friendships with Eliot and Ezra Pound and talked with him enthusiastically about modern poetry. As Cowley followed Aiken's career over the years he understood better a theory of art Aiken first expounded that February of 1918:

I discovered that candor was close to being his central principle as a man and a writer, particularly as a poet. The principle evolved into a system of aesthetics and literary ethics that unified his work, a system based on the private and public value of self-revelation. . . . By finding words for his inmost truth, the writer—especially the poet—has made it part of the world, part of human consciousness. He has become a soldier, so to speak, in the agelong war that mankind has been waging against the subliminal and the merely instinctive.[26]

Cowley understood the full implications of Aiken's theory of art only in retrospect. It was a hybrid of the American literary tradition and French Symbolist notions of artistic isolation and subjectivism. But Aiken's American transformation of Symbolist ideas, his awareness of the "public as opposed to the merely private value of complete self-revelation," separated him from Symbolist hermeticism. Something else about Aiken, however, most impressed Cowley as a young man. In a letter of February 25, 1918, recounting a dinner several days earlier at the Hotel Touraine in Boston, Cowley said that it was Aiken's total dedication

25. Cowley, *And I Worked at the Writer's Trade*, 232.
26. Cowley to Burke, February 17, 25, 1918; Cowley, *And I Worked at the Writer's Trade*, 233–34.

to the life of art that distinguished him. His integrity in dedicating his life single-mindedly to both his art and his family, Cowley announced, had now become Cowley's ideal also.[27]

During much of the spring of 1918 Cowley was busy attempting to keep alive an almost moribund Harvard literary life. Several letters in March described his belief that a new literary magazine free of politics was needed to publish new poets he admired, including Aiken and William Carlos Williams. In April he was elected president of the *Advocate* almost by default, he said, because many student writers had left college for the army. With the help of the few remaining undergraduates interested in literature, Cowley worked to keep the magazine alive. In May the *Advocate* invited Amy Lowell for what turned out to be a raucous and lively meeting. Otherwise the spring was filled with classes and *Advocate* and *Harvard Crimson* drinking parties, where Cowley met new friends, solidified his relations with other young writers, and occasionally got roaring drunk. But Harvard's literary life was becoming too "dilettantish" and raucous for his tastes. He was eager for the company of older friends and also for life in the country.[28]

Early in June, Cowley took a long walking trip with Foster Damon. The trip ended in a tumbledown shack on a hilltop near the village of Candor, in central New York State. A friend in Greenwich Village had told Cowley about the shack, which could be rented—complete with a kitchen stove—for three dollars a month. Kenneth Burke joined them there two or three days later. Before his arrival Damon and Cowley had invented a "plowboy poet" named Earl Roppel and had written his complete poetical works; it was a literary hoax that later achieved some notoriety.[29]

Cowley went to a summer camp that offered a Harvard course

27. Cowley, *And I Worked at the Writer's Trade*, 234; Cowley to Burke, February 25, 1918.
28. Cowley to Burke, March 17, 25, April 27, May 11, 25, 1918.
29. Cowley, *And I Worked at the Writer's Trade*, 39–43.

called Military Science 1. In September he was back at college,
this time in a dormitory transformed into a military barracks. He
enlisted in the army and was sent to Field Artillery Officers Training Corps at Camp Taylor, near Louisville, Kentucky, but his
course there was interrupted by the armistice. His only writing
during those months was a poem called "Bayonet Drill: Two
Sonnets" in collaboration with Damon.[30]

Cowley never returned to wartime Europe. Instead he spent
the winter and spring of 1919 in Greenwich Village because the
demobilization of the army made him half a year late to return to
college classes. In New York he eked out a meager living selling
book reviews while trying to find time to write poems and court a
young New York artist whom he had met during the winter.
Peggy Baird Johns was a divorcee several years older than Cowley,
who aspired to be a painter and worked as aide to a successful
New York graphic illustrator. Through her Cowley was introduced to the commercial art community of New York. During
the spring he moved into Peggy Baird's Greenwich Village apartment and later in the summer of 1919 they were married. This
period of his early years in the Village appears to have had an
important and largely negative impact on Cowley. On the basis of
the little available evidence, Peggy Baird was somewhat undisci-
plined and a true bohemian artist. Over the course of their marriage, which lasted for twelve years, the two slowly grew apart as
Cowley became more and more uncomfortable with her drinking
and her often chaotic personal habits.

The poverty of the first months of marriage and the joint pursuit of careers in the arts made the conditions of living less than
comfortable. Cowley wrote of that time years later when he remembered doing anonymous book reviews for a dollar each. He
also remembered collapsing on a New York street one day in
1919, only later realizing his need for food. Cowley has written

30. *Harvard Advocate*, November, 1918, p. 18.

that the incident made him swallow his pride and, over Peggy's objections, take a low-paying job to pay back the money they had borrowed from friends and buy groceries. During the summer of 1919 he worked for a New York industry magazine, *The Iron Age*, and, when possible, read the French authors he needed to know to keep up with his literary friends. He read Rousseau's *Confessions* and *Madame Bovary* in late June and early July and followed public events by reading the *New Republic*, which had ceased to be regarded as the voice of the Wilson administration. His letters during the early summer indicate that the marginal life he was leading in the unkempt and disorderly society of Greenwich Village, with a wife whose friends seemed to be Village bums as well as artists, began to weigh on Cowley's spirits. In July he wrote in a letter, "And God I am dissatisfied with life."[31]

In an essay he wrote in 1963 describing the chief literary influence on him during that summer of 1919, Cowley stated that the poetry of Jules Laforgue was a subject of study among many of the young American poets of the time, including Foster Damon, Kenneth Burke, Allen Tate, Hart Crane, Louise Bogan, John Brooks Wheelwright, and Yvor Winters. Part of the interest in Laforgue was awakened by Ezra Pound, who had published a long essay on French Symbolist poetry in 1918 in the *Little Review*, which was then being read by young poets as the voice of modern art in America. Pound's essay briefly described and promoted a number of Symbolists, particularly Tristan Corbière and Laforgue, and argued that all good modern poetry derived from the Symbolists.[32] Cowley began studying Laforgue shortly after reading Pound's essay, and by the summer of 1919 he was spending considerable time imitating and, he says, sometimes misreading

31. Cowley, *And I Worked at the Writer's Trade*, 53–54; Cowley to Burke, June 10, July 8, 1919.

32. Cowley, *And I Worked at the Writer's Trade*, 69–81; Ezra Pound, "A Study in French Poets," in Margaret Anderson (ed.), *The Little Review Anthology* (New York, 1953), 164–75.

the rhythms, the urban subject matter, and the ironic attitude of Laforgue's poetry.[33]

The interest in Laforgue, Cowley later wrote, was difficult to explain because few American poets understood much about French prosody. But Laforgue's sensibility, as well as his style, fitted their postwar, somewhat disillusioned adolescence when they suddenly found themselves living in bohemian squalor rather than the clean surroundings of their middle-class youth:

We were impressed by his subject matter. Most of our reading had been among country poets, and Laforgue seemed new to us partly because he was urban. Moreover, we were young and yearning, and we found it exciting to read a poet who regarded adolescence as a time of life that deserved as much serious attention as any other time. He perfectly expressed our feeling about women . . . and we also found confirmation of our instinctive notion about the best means of defending ourselves. The best means was a style, a literary attitude applied to life; it was irony, paradox, and a parade of learning.[34]

Three poems he wrote at this time mirrored these feelings. The poems imitated Laforgue's stanzaic structure, the use of learned and often unusual combinations of words that bordered on sheer linguistic play, and a weary attitude of boredom toward a sordid world of urban squalor. One long poem which Cowley sent to the *Little Review*, perhaps remembering Pound's essay, contained seven stanzas presenting the consciousness of a young bohemian artist:

Sunday in my bedroom staring
Through the broken window pane,
I watch the slanting lines of rain,
And since I have an empty purse
Turn to philosophy again:—

33. Cowley, *And I Worked at the Writer's Trade*, 72.
34. *Ibid.*, 74.

The world is a potato paring,
The refuse of the universe
    And Man excrescent
    Adolescent

Oh for some drunken luxury,
For a divine intoxication,
For love that rises suddenly—
The ordinary dull flirtation
    That lasts a day
    And dies away
Leaves life too barren a sensation. . . .

The concluding stanza follows several other variations on the
dullness of modern life and a modern artist's disillusioned feelings
toward a twentieth-century urban environment:

Boredom that had accumulated
Since Eve and the Pleistocene
    Though belated
    Will be done,
Leaving a constellation clean
    Of grief and schism
    And organism
Lying cold under a cold sun.[35]

  The other two poems, written at this time but not published
until later, imitated Laforgue's style more than his sensibility.
One, called "Nocturne," interrupted with occasional popular
song lyrics a dramatic dialogue of an adolescent girl dreaming of a
gallant young man. The language of the poem again exhibited a
verbal playfulness and an alternating counterpoint of ideas. The
other, which because of its immaturity Cowley did not publish
until years later and then only for historical reasons, was similarly
adolescent in its language and subject matter. It incorporated

---

35. Malcolm Cowley, "Sunday Afternoon: (After Jules Laforgue)," in Anderson (ed.), *Little Review Anthology*, 295–96.

verses of popular music just as Laforgue had. Two stanzas illustrate this point:

As celibates we cerebrate
tonight, we stutter and perplex
our minds with Death and Time and Sex;
we dream of star-sent, heaven-bent
plans for perpetual betterment;
tomorrow morning we shall curse
to find the self-same universe.

        Frankie and Johnny were lovers—
Lordy how those two could love!
They swore to be true to each other,
just as true as the stars above.[36]

In later repudiating the self-indulgent and depressed mood of that poverty-ridden first encounter with artistic bohemia, Cowley nevertheless recognized that his experience had been formative. He wrote about his own "postwar era of disillusion" with evident dislike and self-criticism but also with understanding:

After the war, we drifted to New York, to the district south of Fourteenth street, where one could occupy a hall bedroom for two or three dollars weekly and rent the unfurnished top floor of a rickety dwelling for thirty dollars a month. There were two schools among us: those who painted the floors black (they were the last of the aesthetes) and those who did not paint the floors. Our college textbooks and the complete works of Jules Laforgue gathered dust on the mantelpiece among a litter of unemptied ash-trays. The streets outside were those of Glenn Coleman's early paintings: low, red-brick, early nineteenth-century houses, crazy doorways, sidewalks covered with black snow, and in the foreground, an old woman bending under a sack of rags.

In this setting of dirt and poverty, we passed our post-graduate, postbellum years, scantily clothed, poorly fed, making drafts against our

36. Malcolm Cowley, "Nocturne," *Blue Juniata* (New York, 1929), 37–39; Malcolm Cowley, "Variations on a Cosmical Air," *Blue Juniata: Collected Poems* (New York, 1968), 34–35.

abundant constitutions, and enjoying ourselves almost feverishly. For, there was much in our surroundings that agreed with our mood. We had been born with illusions, unlike the present generation, but having lost them at a very early age, we felt the need of replacing them with others; and we had come to erect the sordid into a kind of religion. We worshipped the cluttered streets, the overflowing ash-cans, the houses full of people and rats; we felt something like veneration for the barrooms then in the last months of their legal existence; and our writings, too, had the smell of sawdust, youth, squalor and Luke O'Connor's beer-and-stout. They had other qualities that were more questionable—a sort of crooked sentiment, a self-protective smirk—yet in a way I respect their emotions, and I like to think that the boy of twenty, the dead adolescent who wrote these seven poems and fifty others like them, has the right to be heard today among his elders and his heirs.[37]

By the end of the summer of 1919 Cowley began to shed the influence of his French literary models. He had decided to return to Harvard for a final semester in order to obtain his degree, and a scholarship made that possible. But first he went home to Belsano and spent a week or two fishing and working in the family yard. When he was finally free of the noise and cramped quarters of New York, his mood sharply changed. The country was his favorite scene, and it always seemed to revive his spirit.

When he returned to Harvard in late September, 1919, he was no longer able to rejoin the social order of students whose lives had not been interrupted by war and whose interests remained collegiate. While his wife remained in New York, Cowley shed his summer despondency. The intellectual environment at Harvard reinvigorated his literary spirits, and his escape from the city also inspired a change in his writing. Several poems he published that fall in *Poetry* magazine reflected this change. They show him turning his attention to the larger literary world. They describe farm scenes and people back in Pennsylvania. Another poem, one that first appeared in the *Harvard Advocate*, describes Boston

37. Cowley, "Note," *Blue Juniata*, 33–34.

summer crowds at the seashore places he had recently observed. One stanza of the Boston poem in particular mirrored the new postwar society:

And now Society comes marching by,
Young Kuppenheimer gods in bathing suits
And flappers with their bonnets stuck
                    awry:—
Sand filters into patent leather boots;

The sun is scorching painted cheeks;
                    the sea
Growls at the littered beach complain-
                    ingly.[38]

The reality of the social and natural world increasingly captured Cowley's attention in his final months at college. The Harvard he encountered in the fall of 1919 was infected by the conservative political reaction of the period immediately after the war. Cowley seems to have been mostly unconcerned by it, living off campus in a furnished room and burdened by an academic overload. Nevertheless, memory of the conservative atmosphere at Harvard remained with him throughout his life. An older Pittsburgh Jewish student, who was a lifelong Cowley friend, bitterly remembered fifty years later the anti-Semitism he felt at Harvard and confessed that Cowley, who had refused to attend his class reunions, was right in doing so. One of Cowley's classmates, an outsider at college but already an established New York businessman when he corresponded with Cowley in the 1920s, questioned him about his vague socialist sympathies at Harvard.[39] Cowley only fully understood the aristocratic, politically conservative aspect of Harvard later in life, although it contributed to

38. "Nantasket," in Culler (ed.), *Harvard Advocate Centennial Anthology*, 113.

39. Jacob Davis to Cowley, June 16, 1959, May 28, 1967; Roy Head to Cowley, n.d., 1926.

his lifelong ambivalence about his college. He loved and remained loyal to the intellectual traditions of the place and the
writer friends he made there, but he mistrusted its social elitism.

Although there is little evidence of any political activity by
Cowley in his college years, he was affected by the antisocialist
backlash of the postwar period. Cowley also seemed to have been
stigmatized as a Bolshevik by some of his classmates, who were
bound for the orthodox world of business, merely because of his
intention to pursue a literary career.[40] His previous residence in
Greenwich Village identified him as a political rebel. Yet his
mild interest in socialism, apparently learned in 1919 from
reading men such as Van Wyck Brooks in journals like the *Seven
Arts*, was always overwhelmed by his personal absorption in
aesthetic matters. Any political consciousness he developed resulted from Harvard's, and America's, political reaction rather
than from any developing social "alienation." Poetry, not politics,
consumed his interest.

By January, 1920, at the end of his last semester at Harvard,
Cowley seemed anxious to leave college and Boston behind him.
His literary interests were already focused on the wider world,
particularly New York. His friend Kenneth Burke had dropped
out of Columbia to pursue his writing career full time, and a
number of Harvard graduates interested in art had moved to New
York. In January two of those men, James Sibley Watson and
Scofield Thayer, both millionaires, bought a conventional political and literary journal, the *Dial*, and began to transform it into a
lively publication dedicated to publishing the best of New York
contemporary works of and about the arts. Kenneth Burke became associated with the magazine in its first month and was paid
one hundred dollars for a story he submitted.[41] Cowley himself
had, through a friend of his wife's, been given several books to
review for the old *Dial*. One of those reviews was the only mate-

40. Malcolm Cowley, in conversation with the author, July, 1975.
41. Cowley to Burke, January 26, 1920.

rial from the old magazine approved for publication by the new editors. Cowley's Harvard background encouraged Thayer and Watson to give him several other books to review during the spring.[42]

Those reviews demonstrate the beginnings of a clearly articulated aesthetic theory. It was a theory that seemed to emerge abruptly, for nowhere in his previous writings did he betray such a sharp sense of what was wrong with the aestheticism of modern art. Three of the five reviews he published in the spring of 1920 in the *Dial* and the *New Republic* evidenced this criticism. One in particular, of two novels by Sheila Kaye-Smith written in England after the war, indicated his antiaestheticism:

Modern art subsists to a remarkable extent by taking in its own washing. Novelists adopt poets for heroes, who write sonnets on pictures, for which musicians compose orchestral settings. Painters contribute fantastic portraits of all these folks and become in turn the heroes of new novels: the circle is complete. Think over the list of Mr. Cannan's chief characters, or Miss Sinclair's, or Romain Rolland's. It is true of course that an occasional hero is free from the taint of art: he is always different, however, from the mass of men, having at least the artistic sensibilities. Sometimes an author dives into the sea of life and grasps an authentic, unliterary experience: at such occasions we have reason to be grateful. Sheila Kaye-Smith has made the plunge and returned tightly clutching a bit of soil.[43]

In a review in the April *Dial*, Cowley turned his attack on Romain Rolland: "Rolland is a monumental architect, however, not an intaglio worker or even a sculptor. He feels a sense of limitation in three hundred pages, and splashes through them a little awkwardly, like an elephant in a bathtub."[44]

42. Introduction, in Diane U. Eisenberg, *Malcolm Cowley: A Checklist of His Writings, 1916–1973* (Carbondale, 1975), xv–xvi.

43. Malcolm Cowley, "The Woman of Ihornden," *Dial*, LXX (February, 1920), 259–62.

44. Malcolm Cowley, "Colas Breugnon," *Dial*, LXX (April, 1920), 513–16.

Cowley's own developing aesthetic and his new antiaestheticism appear in a review of the war poetry of Siegfried Sassoon that he wrote in New York in the late spring of 1920. He praised Sassoon for a poetry of historical and social criticism rather than romantic subjectivism and escapist lyricism:

When a poet like Siegfried Sassoon tries . . . to talk about something else than nightingales and the trees and meadows which are their haunt; when he goes back to Donne and Swift instead of the Elizabethan lyricists, he has to struggle against a whole tradition of vapidity. He is fighting—whether or not consciously—for the theory of poetry as a mature art, as against the theory which would attach poetry definitely to the childhood of the race and the individual. Too much of contemporary verse expresses the emotions of a girl of twelve in words of one syllable. . . . Sassoon is an alien among them [the Georgians]; he started with one poetic virtue—honesty—and that was unqualifiedly positive. . . . One regrets that the collection of his war poems is not arranged chronologically, with separate dates for beginning and middle and end. For one thing, such an arrangement would determine whether he wrote before Barbusse or afterwards.[45]

These early reviews indicated that Malcolm Cowley, like so many other literary figures of his generation, entered the postwar era to confront the school of Paris. But unlike his peers, Cowley went to Greenwich Village and the School of Paris in the early 1920s only to discover the school of classical humanism and nature.

45. Malcolm Cowley, "Against Nightingales," *Dial*, LXX (May, 1920), 621–25.

CHAPTER 3

Greenwich Village, 1920–1921

When Malcolm Cowley arrived in New York in February, 1920, the city's cultural life was undergoing a radical transformation. In the years before World War I artists and writers in New York had often related their work to the particular social and political concerns of the Progressive era; by the 1920s they had broadened their interests into what Frederick Lewis Allen described as "pervasive cultural revolt." The revolt was directed at the entire fabric of American social beliefs and moral premises, which had been elevated into a folklore of behavior.[1]

As another historian of the period has written, protest has been endemic among American artists and intellectuals, but never before had there been such a complete antagonism between American artists and the general public. A full-scale "war between the country and the city," between New York as a center of new social values and rural America as an anachronism, represented a momentous shift in American demographic, economic, and political organization.[2] The rigidity of opposition between the two social groups resulted in gross oversimplification of social realities by both sides and intolerance that resulted in confusion and misunderstanding.

Because Malcolm Cowley was an artist and intellectual who migrated to New York's bohemian community in the early 1920s,

1. Frederick Lewis Allen, *Only Yesterday* (1931; rpr. New York, 1964).
2. William E. Leuchtenberg, *The Perils of Prosperity, 1914–1932* (Chicago, 1958), 225–40.

and because he wrote a classic description of the postwar era's philosophy of experimental sexual, social, and aesthetic revolt which originated in Greenwich Village, he has sometimes been identified as a social revolutionary.[3] Yet a study of the sparse record of Cowley's third and longest experience in the Village (a year and a half) shows that he perceived himself as living there so he could get work, not to oppose the culture of the small town or the Bible Belt. When he wrote about the "Village ethic" of self-indulgent individualism a decade after his own experiences there, he described the Village as Frederick Lewis Allen had. Both men wrote in the early 1930s that the Village was different during the 1920s than it had been before the Great War, when its intellectuals held liberal political and social values that were not widely accepted in America. Indeed, Cowley wrote that by the mid-1920s a cultural and social revolt that had begun as a rebellion by a relatively small group of artists ended by having its cultural values and social behavior patterns imitated all across America. Cowley described himself as "simply a young [man] on the make, the humble [citizen] not of Bohemia but of Grub Street."[4]

Cowley seems to have wanted to distinguish his personal experience from that of both the prewar Village radicals and the postwar bohemians. The record of his life in New York from February, 1920, to July, 1921, confirms that it was pursuit of the "writer's trade" that brought him to the Village. Indeed, his preoccupation with scratching out a living appears to have made him mildly indifferent to the larger political, social, and aesthetic revolutions occurring around him.

By June, 1920, Cowley and his wife had settled into a small apartment at 88 West Third Street in the Village. Letters written

3. Dore Ashton, *The New York School* (New York, 1973), 16, cites Cowley as "one of the Village's most intelligent progeny," implying that he was in accord with the Village ethic of revolt from American middle-class standards.

4. Malcolm Cowley, *Exile's Return: A Literary Odyssey of the Nineteen Twenties* (New York, 1951), 65, 73.

at the time show that he already saw the Village as a magnet for fakirs and eccentrics. For example, he described two older Harvard writers he had recently met who were longtime Greenwich Village residents:

Joe Gould is sitting behind me telling Peggy how he plans to go to the farm of the Self Masters tomorrow and be given free board. . . . He has grown a T-shaped moustache and beard, is very thin and seems to be straining ever nearer to insanity. He was almost the medium of my making friends with Estlin Cummings: we met on the street and commiserated ourselves about Joe for half an hour. That day I had decided I must become more than an acquaintance of Estlin's: people who are producing anything are so rare in this town.[5]

Gould, a longtime friend of Cummings, became one of the most notorious residents of the Village and eventually did go insane. He seems to have represented for Cowley the eccentricity of Village life, of artists with little talent pursuing immortality. Gould's unpublished work, for example, "A History of Our Time from Oral Sources," reached "seven feet high" and contained at one time "11,000,000 words," a monument of "documentary art" recording the sleazy life of bohemian rebels and private egocentrism. It was an obsessive attempt to equate one person's emotional history with the history of the world.[6]

Joe Gould is the subject of an entertaining book by Joseph Mitchell, *Joe Gould's Secret*, expanded from a profile in the *New Yorker*. Unfortunately, Mitchell does not deal with Gould's early years in New York, having failed to consult those who knew him then. Joseph Ferdinand Gould "matriculated from Harvard" (in William Slater Brown's phrase); he had started with the class of 1911 but did not finish his freshman year. He came to Greenwich Village and formed the grandiose project of writing what he called "A History of Our Time from Oral Sources." He listened

5. Cowley to Burke, June 4, 1920.
6. Charles Norman, *e. e. cummings: The Magic Maker* (Boston, 1972), 134.

to stories about famous people and took notes. From the years 1920–1921, Cowley remembers reading several of the greasy notebooks that he always carried. In the late 1920s Gould became mildly insane. He partly recovered his wits but never went back to work on his big project, except in fancy. At some point he lost all but two or three of the notebooks. He continued to carry these around and, as Mitchell records at length, used them as an excuse for cadging drinks. Greenwich Village lost some of its smell and savor when Joe Gould was carried off to a state hospital.

To Cowley, Gould seemed to symbolize the weird culture of Village society, which increasingly appeared to him full of charlatans, frauds, and pseudo-artists. In a letter of June 9, for example, he described the boozy, crazy atmosphere of Village parties in the summer of 1920. The impression he received was of a surreal world in which strange people, intoxicated and often acting irrationally, drifted in and out of rooms. At one party he met a millionaire couple who had set up a loft in the Village, in addition to their country estate, in order to imitate the bohemian style of "abstract painters" and experiment with bisexualism.[7]

Cowley's reaction to this Village eccentricity was to plan to escape it as soon as he could afford to. While the rebels of the Village celebrated freedom from the "puritan" restraints of rural America, Cowley dreamed of returning to the country. He wrote Burke:

[My] idea is one that Peggy and I have worked out, and it should suit you as well as it does us. I decided against regular commuting, but around Haverstraw there is regular farming country and it is within thirty-five miles of 42nd street. Why not rent a house for ten or fifteen a month—it can be done—and live there during the summer, or perhaps during the whole year and raise a large vegetable garden. Peggy plans also to sell flowers. The little money necessary for existence can be raised through a carefully cultivated typewriter and one or two trips a week to

7. Cowley to Burke, June 9, 1920; Joseph Mitchell, *Joe Gould's Secret* (New York, 1965).

the city. Think it over. It combines the best features of the plans we
have talked over. Mountains, woods, groundhogs, trout, literature. If
we are to undertake this vita nuova it will begin next spring very early.[8]

But during the remaining months of 1920 Cowley had to work
as a copywriter for *Sweet's Architectural Catalogue* in order to support himself and his wife. He found his job unchallenging and
boring but legitimate in that he did not need to compromise his
integrity to sell shoddy products. He could write copy so fast that
when not required to read the latest issue of the *American Machin-
ist*, he had time to write poems. And his poetry in 1920 reflected
his ambivalent attitude toward his own career. He was torn
between his ambition to be a professional writer, which would
require living in New York, and his personal desire to create a
community of artists in the country, where he could live and still
be a professional writer: "The project of living in the country," he
wrote Burke on June 19, "seems buried temporarily; till next
Spring at least. My idea was never communal living; I don't
approve of that. We might run a community garden but the
houses should be separate. We shouldn't have much trouble in
accomplishing the whole adventure. Keep it in mind."[9]

The continuous discussion and sometimes ludicrous misunderstanding among the friends about a community of artists reveal
Cowley's seriousness about finding another social option for
American artists in an era when university teaching positions or
such places as the Yaddo or MacDowell colonies did not exist.
And also it helps explain why later in life Cowley devoted much
of his time to creating and administering those rural institutions
of art so that subsequent generations of artists would not have to
live in urban ghettos.

Like any Grub Street hack, Cowley had to write, mostly in the
evenings and on weekends, on subjects that were generally not of

8. *Ibid.*
9. *Ibid.*, June 19, 1920.

his choosing. Most of his published writing during the fall of
1920 was for the weekly literary supplement of the New York
Evening Post; the books he was given to review focused his attention all across the subject matter of contemporary book publishers. In the issue of October 2, for example, he reviewed a book by
a French writer, Mary Duclaux, on the history and changing
cultural conditions of twentieth-century France. In other fall
issues of the *Post's* weekend literary supplement he reviewed *Three
Plays of the Argentine* edited by Edward Bierstadt, *Youth and
Egolatry* by Pio Baroja, and *The World's Timber* by Alexander L.
Howard. For the issue of December 31, he reviewed a translation
of the diaries of noblewomen of the court of Japan in the Middle
Ages and books of plays and poems by Alfred Kreymborg and
Haniel Long.[10]

The most interesting of Cowley's reviews in the fall of 1920
dealt with Edith Sitwell's *Wheels*, the poetry annual that appeared
between 1916 and 1921. Through these anthologies, which
a literary historian years ago described as "premonitory of the
nineteen-twenties," the Sitwells intended to place themselves
at the center of the London literary attack on the vulgarity of
modern life and culture. Their foremost object was "to rouse
public interest by deliberate eccentricity and aggressive self-
advertisement," to "épater la bourgeoisie."[11]

Cowley connected the works in *Wheels* with the sensibility
of the "decadent" writers associated with London's *Yellow Book*
artists of the 1890s. He contrasted the eccentricity of the Sitwells

10. Malcolm Cowley, "Mme. Duclaux on France," New York *Evening Post
Literary Review*, October 2, 1920, p. 3; "Gaucho Drama," *ibid.*, November 13,
1920, p. 3; "The Era of Disillusion," *ibid.*, November 20, 1920, p. 4; "The
World's Timber," *ibid.*, November 27, 1920, p. 4; "Woman of Japan," *ibid.*,
December 24, 1920, p. 9; "Entertaining Plays," *ibid.*, December 31, 1920,
p. 5; "Motley Verse," *ibid.*, December 31, 1920, p. 9.

11. Samuel C. Chew, "The Nineteenth Century and After: 1789–1939," in
Albert C. Baugh (ed.), *A Literary History of England* (New York, 1948), 1579–
80, 1584.

with the mannered style of the Georgian poetry anthologies of sentimental rusticity and innocent gentility which he had read in college: "[The Sitwell phenomenon] represents one of the two or three important developments in English poetry during the last decade—a strange commentary on the literary importance of one family. . . . The simplicity of the Georgians had begun some years ago to develop into a fixed and imitable mannerism; from that time on the reaction was inevitable. Its form, its content, and the exact date of its occurrence were determined by the irruption of the Sitwell family into the circle of the [Georgian] poets." [12]

The Sitwells reacted strongly against the Georgians with a new poetic of self-exaggerated ostentation and by displaying eclectic styles of art. By the early 1920s their practice, along with that of Pound and Eliot, changed poetry in England into a "modern" style of "obscure, experimental," antididactic, and "anti-social" private languages for coteries. Cowley sensed that the anthology represented a new outbreak of what he described as the "disease" of the decadent writers of the 1890s: "The malady of the nineties has attacked them in a much less malignant form: it is even so modified that scientists might call it a new disease." [13]

Cowley's writings during his year in New York show that he saw himself as an apprentice journalist forced to struggle in a debilitating environment. He put up with it, however, in the hope that his experience would lead eventually to fulfillment of his ambition, a life as a professional writer existing modestly but comfortably in the country. On August 25, 1920, he wrote Burke,

But this fit of Viennese melancholy, this lavender-and-old-rose regret for other days, grows simply out of inability to adjust to my financial

12. Malcolm Cowley, "Georgians and Post-Georgians," *New Republic*, September 15, 1920, pp. 77–78.

13. Chew, "Nineteenth Century and After," : 583; Cowley, "Georgians and Post-Georgians," 77–78.

condition. This week Peggy lost seven dollars, and as a result I had to hock our cameos and wrap the pawn ticket carefully around the fountain pen ticket and the ticket for my Phi Beta Kappa key. Contrast this situation ludicrously with yours. Soon my salary goes up to fifty: I am to get ten a week extra from the *Post* for handling their briefer stuff, and yet I bet I am still the width of a bank vault from the nearest savings account. And therefore I continue to work on an architectural catalogue. . . . On the subject of finances: I hope you don't wait till November or thereabouts. I can get you plenty to do for *Export Trade*, and unless something unforeseen happens, I can turn you over my ten-a-week job on the *Post*. After counting checks, I found that I actually earned between forty and fifty a week as a freelance, and it was only my inability to stick it out that dished me. You still have a little capital, and there is no reason that you should go back to thirty per in the movie business. And by the way, if you need a place to [live] until such time as you find an apartment, Peggy and I have a five-room house in the country to offer you. We pay only ten a month.[14]

His hopes for 1921 were to prove unfounded. His offer of help to Kenneth Burke was indicative of his optimistic personality. But in 1921, in Greenwich Village, Cowley had enough to do to keep himself fed.

The winter of 1921 appears to have had a lasting negative effect on Cowley. The cold of New York increased his growing disenchantment. For months he was unable to write poetry, and the only poem he published between August of 1920 and December of 1921 was a narrative describing life in a country farmhouse. The poem, titled "About Seven O'Clock," captured the languorous life of a lost nineteenth-century world. Some of the poem's imagery may in part have also figuratively expressed Cowley's dry spirit:

About seven o'clock, when they have wiped the
                            last of the supper dishes
the housewives of Altamont emerge on their front
                                                porches,

14. Cowley to Burke, August 25, 1920.

selecting rocking chairs
they sway, rhythmically:
one . . . two (and the soles of their shoes tap the
floor)
one . . . two.

Today it is very hot. Yesterday
there wasn't a cloud in the sky.
Rain tomorrow, maybe, and cooler weather after.
July—in the eighteen-seventies or nineteen-ten
or fifty years from now, it doesn't matter:
one . . . two (and their shoes beat out the meter
on the porch floor)

till at half-past nine
the housewives climb to the front bedroom with
their oil lamps:
in all the houses of the Great Valley at half-past
nine
shadows mount fantastically over the flowered paper
of the hallways
there is the rustle of gingham up narrow stairs. [15]

The five book reviews Cowley published between January 1, 1921, and his departure for France in midsummer revealed a mind already impatient with the literary tendencies of the early 1920s. For example, a January *Dial* review of a book of poems by Aldous Huxley gave Cowley the opportunity to criticize a tendency of modern writing he described as adolescent Romanticism, the egoistic indulgence of private sensibility, and the equally egoistic refusal to face the contemporary world:

Leda is a book of adolescence: its author recognizes this fact explicitly. . . . A chinless age, Aldous Huxley goes on to call the period (He uses his own words this time); an age feebly skeptical, inefficient, profoundly unhappy. In other words it is the stage at which one measures the traditional precepts into which one has been educated against

15. Malcolm Cowley, "About Seven O'Clock," New York *Evening Post Literary Review*, January 22, 1921, p. 7.

the immoral realities of experience; depending on which force proves the stronger, one becomes idealist or realist.[16]

The conclusion of the review reflected Cowley's own experience, for he saw in Huxley a portrait of the disillusioned intellectuals who had been uprooted by the war and the industrial, urbanizing forces of the postwar period. Cowley argued that a good many contemporary artists had chosen a third practice rather than the two he called cynically realist or romantically idealist. That third practice was a perpetuation of adolescent self-infatuation. He argued that it was Jules Laforgue and the French Symbolist sensibility that had encouraged young artists in this direction, and he urged Huxley to move on to other subjects and more mature emotions, to let his book stand as an obituary to a dead adolescence. The essay may have reflected Cowley's own psychology more than Huxley's (Huxley became a major voice of the London modernist movement in the 1920s), and it was clearly Cowley who wished to put his adolescence behind him.

In the spring of 1921, in a long review of two volumes of poems by his old Boston friends Conrad Aiken and John Gould Fletcher, Cowley criticized the rising tide of experimentalism in modern art. Part of his essay rebutted criticism of Aiken by Babette Deutsch, who had commented in an essay in the March *Dial* that Aiken was too imitative a poet. Cowley argued that mature poets had always borrowed from and been influenced by other poets. Originality of style as an absolute goal, he said, only impoverishes the rich traditions of art. A study of poets demonstrates that poetry is not the result of isolated inspiration. Such a study

would [prove] that poets learn from their contemporaries as well as from their predecessors—a fact which one could have verified more easily from readings in Shakespeare and Marlowe, or from a study of Dorothy Wordsworth's diary.

16. Malcolm Cowley, "The Chinless Age," *Dial*, LXX (January, 1921), 73–76.

And yet it is a fact which the more romantic members of the present generation (in other words, the majority) are striving vigorously to forget. Behind Miss Deutsch's attack on Conrad Aiken there lay an idea of a totally different sort: namely, that poems may spring, fully adorned, from the forehead of any casual Jove. Put in another way, it is the idea of the poet as a modern St. Simeon Stylites, who, standing aloof on a pillar, draws masterpieces from the wells of the Inner Consciousness.

The whole question of authorship and originality has been ridiculously overemphasized during the last century. The results are upon us in an epidemic of bad grammar and bad workmanship, and curiously enough, in a great deal of unconscious plagiarism.

Far better for the imitation to be conscious. The poet is a workman to whom a certain task has been set, and it is no dishonour if he calls on his fellows to aid him. Or he might be compared more specifically to a builder at work on the unfinished nave or the portion of a wall, and passes on; the important question is not his identity but whether he has done his work well. The workman who succeeds him builds further upon what has already been constructed, as Laforgue built on Baudelaire and as T. S. Eliot has built on Laforgue. There are periods of general demolition—and they are very necessary—in which the false work of several generations is torn down, but never is one forced to begin again on new foundations. For to be completely original, one would have to invent a language of one's own; even the idiom in which we work is a sort of crystallized poetry. . . . These things are banal, but they are irritatingly true.

Aiken and Fletcher recognize their truth; that is why these borrowings back and forth are significant. In a generation so proud of its independence that it gets nowhere, they have been content, for a little while, to work together towards a common aim.[17]

This review seems to indicate that Cowley was already struggling with what he later came to believe was an impossible quest of modern art, from Mallarmé's search for a purified language to modern painters' completely new expressive idiom, the attempt

17. Malcolm Cowley, "These Things Are Banal . . . ," *Dial*, LXX (June, 1921), 700–704.

to escape the rational accretions of language which accumulated centuries had deposited. The desire for a primal, primitive language in words was one symptom of that quest, and Cowley could not accept it. Part of his understanding of the impossibility of the Symbolist quest for a pure language had come from his friend Kenneth Burke's researches in French Symbolist prose and poetry. In the February *Dial*, Burke had published an essay (later reflected in his essay on Remy de Gourmont in *Counter-Statement*) stating that the poetic of the Symbolists could be summarized as "the reduction to absurdity of individualism in art [so as to] spend one's life in talking to oneself." [18] Even more than Burke, Cowley in his developing idea of art emphasized the traditions of aesthetic communication.

The spring of 1921 seems to have been a time of personal crisis for Cowley. His New York life was increasingly oppressive. Also, the April *Dial* contained a long essay by Ernest Boyd angrily critical of the New York Society for the Suppression of Vice and its legal efforts to censor Joyce's *Ulysses*, the *Little Review*, and James Branch Cabell's best-selling fantasy novel *Jurgen*, which apparently added to Cowley's unhappiness with New York. Cowley had talked with his Boston friend John Wheelwright in early May, and both men admitted a sense of helplessness in the face of the powerful reactionary forces of the Harding years. In addition, in early May Cowley had suddenly been forced to return to Pittsburgh because his father was ill. He stayed at home until his father recovered some weeks later. While in Pittsburgh he sold his piano for $250 to help pay off personal debts in New York and provide funds to last through June. [19] His Grub Street existence had not improved; poverty and debt seemed constant. By June of 1921 finding an alternative to this condition was his dominant purpose.

18. Kenneth Burke, "Approaches to Remy de Gourmont," *Dial*, LXX (February, 1921), 125–38.
19. Cowley to Burke, May 5, 1921.

The exodus of American artists to Europe had begun in earnest during the spring, and Cowley, seemingly always a step behind and a follower, was increasingly interested in the possibility of returning to France. His last review in New York for the *Post* was of a book on American foreign policy and the "liberal" program for a postwar international politics.[20]

But his last months in New York during 1921 reveal once again the paradox of his early years. While criticizing modern art for its insularity and apparent lack of social concern, Cowley left America to confront in full force the energies of European modern art. His experience in France was to be most influential for his early development. But as Samuel Johnson never forgot the wretched writers of eighteenth-century London, Cowley never lost the memory of his Grub Street experience.[21]

20. Malcolm Cowley, "A Liberal Policy," New York *Evening Post Literary Review*, July 9, 1921, p. 5.

21. John Wain, *Samuel Johnson: A Biography* (New York, 1975), 100–131.

CHAPTER 4

Paris and Encounters with the European Avant-Garde

Malcolm Cowley's journey to Paris in the early 1920s, like those of many of his contemporaries, appears to have been motivated by a combination of personal reasons, and these were not as simple as some later cultural critics have made them appear. Indeed, the motives behind the American artistic exodus of the 1920s remain ambiguous, clouded by the contradictory testimony of the members of the Lost Generation and by the prejudices of their critics. To Alfred Kazin, for example, viewing the 1920s from the political perspective of the 1930s, the artists of the Lost Generation were unique because of their "aristocratic alienation." Their profound "disenchantment" with American life became the great subject of their art, and their allegiance to the ideals of European modern art distinguished them from all other generations of American artists.[1]

Yet many of these artists viewed their Paris years differently from Kazin. Books like Sylvia Beach's *Shakespeare and Company* or Matthew Josephson's *Life Among the Surrealists* explain the allure of Paris as owing principally to its convivial hospitality to art and artists. Both Beach and Josephson implied that although the American expatriates were inspired by European modern artists, many of them also remained deeply interested in American culture. Josephson's book describes a gradual disillusionment with the doctrines and behavior of European literary and visual artists.[2]

1. Alfred Kazin, *On Native Grounds* (1942; rpr. New York, 1956), 240–41.
2. Sylvia Beach, *Shakespeare and Company* (New York, 1956); Matthew Josephson, *Life Among the Surrealists* (New York, 1962).

Even the most famous of the American expatriate writers of the
1920s left an ambiguous record of his experience. The Hemingway of *The Sun Also Rises* provided a much more cynical and critical portrayal of Paris than did the Hemingway of *A Moveable
Feast*. For Cowley, too, at least so far as can be determined on the
basis of the available evidence, Paris was an ambiguous encounter, one both rich in its encouragement of his artistic interests and
disturbing in the understanding which Cowley finally carried
home with him.

Cowley's Grub Street routine in Greenwich Village, dividing
his hours between writing poems, reviewing books, and working
full time as copywriter for architectural and engineering catalogs,
left him little time for reflective thought and serious study of art.
By the summer of 1921 the confinement of Manhattan also seemed
to weigh heavily on his spirit. His retreats to the countryside
were not numerous enough to overcome his feeling of oppression
in the city.

In late June he wrote a long letter to Kenneth Burke which
mentioned a number of New York artists who had already left
New York for Paris because of Warren G. Harding's "normalcy,"
Prohibition, and the increasing activities of the Society for the
Suppression of Vice. He confessed that he was unhappy and frus-
trated with both his routine job and his inability to pursue his
intellectual interests: "I have been unhappy—alas. I am unhappy— alas, alas. I don't know what it is; it resembles more
than anything else the mal du siècle of the Romantics. One gets
up, putters around the house, the office . . . goes to bed. One
tells a client professionally about a boom in building that one
doesn't believe in—and while waiting for his reply wonders when
the devil it is going to end."[3]

A few days later Cowley sent Burke a card announcing that
Alfred Kreymborg, an established New York poet, was soliciting
material for a new little magazine, *Broom*, that was soon to begin

3. Cowley to Burke, June 17, 1921.

publishing from Europe.⁴ Cowley seems to have felt that the opportunities to do serious work and find time to pursue his intellectual interests were better in Europe than in New York. He applied to the American Field Service, his old ambulance organization, for a graduate fellowship to study in France, and with the help of John Livingston Lowes he received one to study at the University of Montpellier. By July of 1921 he had joined the exodus of American artists and writers to France. His motive for leaving America, then, was not a total rejection of American culture, as was the case with writers such as Harold Stearns. In the early 1920s America did not provide the freedom and economic support serious artists and intellectuals required.

Before leaving for Paris he submitted to the *Dial* several book reviews which he had completed in June. In one, treating A. E. Coppard's *Adam and Eve and Pinch Me*, which appeared in July, Cowley again attacked what he called the neurasthenic sensibility of modern art. Coppard, Cowley said, had made the "necessary compromise with the imperfections of the actual" that his Romantic forebears could not (and that Cowley himself was having trouble making). Coppard's stories, Cowley wrote, revealed a beauty marked by technical restraint:

Coppard has avoided the Bovarisme of the present generation, which depends on neurosis rather than on a false romance. If Emma were a contemporary of ours, she would dissolve her vapors by attending fashionable psychiatrists, and would return home to write poems in free verse beginning, "I am tired of" . . . or "I hate people who." . . . It is to her modern prototypes that we are indebted for the novel of nerves and for the development of the cult of the disagreeable. Coppard is not healthier, perhaps, but he is saner: He has nerves, but he does not allow them to be rasped continually. . . . He is a careful workman and a sure workman, and a pleasant reminder that the short story, unlike the autobiographical novel, is not yet a dead form.⁵

4. *Ibid.*, June 24, 1921.
5. Malcolm Cowley, "Adam and Eve and Pinch Me," *Dial*, LXXI (July, 1921), 93–95.

In his review of Amy Lowell's *Legends*, which appeared in the
August *Dial*, Cowley extolled Lowell's ability to use myths from
a variety of folklore and to add her own musical effects to the
narrative tales. He particularly applauded Lowell's "honesty" in
admitting to rearranging, adding, mixing, and jumbling the
base story for her own uses: "Writing honestly she could do
nothing else."[6]

A recurring theme of Cowley's criticism was becoming apparent in these reviews. He admired the use of traditional forms, of
subjects other than private emotions, and the honesty of writers
in practicing the craft of writing as it had been handed down to
them. He also admired originality and individuality in material
but not in technique. The Lowell review ended with a detailed
discussion of the poet's technical skills, by which Cowley seems
to have intended to redress his earlier, private ridicule of her work
when he was in college.

At times I was very unjust: in a city of literary failures one mistrusts
established reputations. I have come to believe that one's estimate of
Miss Lowell is bound up with one's estimate of American poetry in
general. The new and excellent qualities of our literature are abundantly
represented in her work, as is also our national tendency to be ragged.
We must wait till the indefinite time when American literature has been
judged before judging her. She is, at any rate, one of the three graces or
nine muses upon whom our poetry stands or falls.[7]

By early July Cowley was writing from 9 rue de Fleurus in
Paris, the location of the American University Union. He described the benefit to him of life on board ship during his Atlantic crossing: "I really should sum up New York for myself if I
want to kill it in my mind, otherwise it will live on like Harvard—and it was a much more unpleasant experience than Harvard College and needs more definite punctuation." The forced

6. Malcolm Cowley, "Programme Music," *Dial*, LXXI (August, 1921),
222–26.
7. *Ibid.*

relaxation on the ship had been good for him and had helped clear away the memory of the bohemian life in the Village: "I needed these days of absolute idleness to remove all trace of New York." And his early impression of the art colony of Paris made him see a parallel between the Village and the Latin Quarter:

Paris, as you may imagine by putting two together with two, has an American colony. That colony centers at the Rotonde, and at times straggles over to Boudet's. Members of that colony, when asked the location of the Louvre and of Montmartre, said, "Anybody can tell you where the Louvre is and nobody goes to Montmartre." They don't go either place. They dine at Boudet's and sleep with one another, or, if they are not homosexual with the tarts of the Quarter. It is Greenwich Village, only much more so than the Village.[8]

The invasion of the Quarter by Americans had begun in 1918, he noted. His disdain for the moral license of the two art colonies, consistent with his conservative reaction in New York, did not coincide with conventional views of the typical avant-garde artist. Indeed, he viewed the job of an artist as one of professional discipline and all his life disliked people who use the "Greenwich Village" behavior pattern as an excuse to indulge their laziness.

During September Cowley spent time in Dijon, boarding with a French family and finishing an essay about the literary interests of his own postwar generation. This essay he sent back to New York for possible publication.[9]

By October Cowley was settled in Montpellier for the beginning of his classes at the university. He was uncertain about the courses he was to take but felt that he was recovering his old days in high school, where he had been free to think, read, and question at his leisure. A letter he received in early October from James Sibley Watson of the *Dial* informed him that Stewart Mitchell, another Harvard writer, would soon be studying at Montpellier. Watson added that he had forwarded several of Cow-

8. Cowley to Burke, July 12, n.d., July 13, August 10, 1921.
9. *Ibid.*, September 17, 1921.

ley's poems to Amy Lowell to see whether the *Dial* should use them.[10]

Meanwhile, Cowley's article on his literary generation was printed in the New York *Evening Post* as a front-page lead in its October 15 *Literary Review*, a new supplement edited by Henry Seidel Canby. In the article Cowley tried to sum up some general characteristics of the work, experience, and literary interests of the young men he had associated with in Boston and New York. Cowley pointed out the differences between the tastes and subject matter of his generation of writers, including particularly their deep interest in modern French art and the nineteenth-century French avant-garde writers from Flaubert and Baudelaire to Remy de Gourmont, and the social and political interests of such older New York writers as Sherwood Anderson. He also suggested that the chief concern of the younger men was the new modern aesthetic, with its emphasis on T. S. Eliot's ideal of "formalism and strangeness" in art. The lack of social concern among a number of young writers whose work Cowley had been following differentiated them, he also wrote, from such prewar English writers as George Bernard Shaw and H. G. Wells. Paris, not London, was the new ideal. The essay was, in fact, a good summary of the aesthetic interests of those writers of whom Cowley was personally aware from his experience in college and from reading the new literary journals, interests with which by then he himself was less than satisfied. Over a decade later the substance of this essay became a section of *Exile's Return*. Without knowing it, he had already begun to write that book.[11]

By the end of October he began to receive letters from New

10. James Sibley Watson to Cowley, October 14, 1921.
11. Malcolm Cowley, "This Youngest Generation," New York *Evening Post Literary Review*, October 15, 1921, pp. 81–82; Cowley, *Exile's Return: A Literary Odyssey of the Nineteen Twenties* (New York, 1951), 97–100. Cowley also later noted that this essay began his lifelong role as chronicler of the Lost Generation (*A Second Flowering: Works and Days of the Lost Generation* [New York, 1974], viii).

York and Boston on his recent work. A long letter from Amy Lowell, discussing the poems Watson had sent her for the *Dial*, provided Cowley some interesting criticism of his recent poetry:

> I do not believe there is very much hope about my placing many of these poems. It is very difficult indeed to find magazines to put this type of poetry into, as you know. Also, I am going to venture a little criticism, if you will let me. Some of the poems are dangerously like prose; in other words, they are not quite rhythmical enough to carry themselves obviously over to the poetic side of literature. I hope you will not mind my saying this, but really perhaps it would be well to keep in mind when you are writing poetry. . . .
>
> You say that you quake in your boots fearing that I shall not like the poems. I do like many of them, but I can see just what, in more than one case, would lift the poem up to the emotional, imaginative, and rhythmical level necessary to turn it into something very fine. It is exactly this teasing a poem up, and then teasing it up some more, until you have wrung the final essence out of it, all the subject will bear and all its implications, which is what I think you need most to learn.[12]

The analysis was shrewd and pointed to a characteristic of Cowley's later poetry. His poems often attempted to capture the conversational idiom of the characters he was representing. In fact, Cowley apparently intended, both in his poetry and in other literary work, to represent the reality of human social life. This practice was evident in a story he wrote at the same time as his poem, based on his transatlantic voyage, which he published in early October in an obscure Paris avant-garde magazine.[13]

Meanwhile, his relationship with Amy Lowell was helping to crack the resistance of the literary journals to his poetry. In late November, Lowell finally placed one of his poems in the *Dial*. She wrote that she was disappointed not to have placed more.[14] The poem, "Mountain Valley," was printed in the December

12. Amy Lowell to Cowley, October 28, 1921.

13. Malcolm Cowley, "The Journey to Paris," *Gargoyle*, I (October, 1921), 8–12.

14. Amy Lowell to Cowley, November 21, 1921.

issue. The setting once again mirrored the Pennsylvania country from which Cowley seemed to derive his most persistent poetic inspiration. It was a dramatic poem using a farmer as voice.

Lost in a mountain valley, we have struggled
for bread too long. Here corn is sparse and blighted.
The valley is too narrow. We have driven
our plows against the stony flanks of the hill.

No use to struggle further, O my brothers;
here in our fields lie down together, rest,

and some day when the earth has grown as cold
as craters in the moon, when falls the sun
black through perpetual twilight, then our hills
will fold like wrinkles in a forehead, press
the valley out between them like slow fingers
against the thumb of Saturn, and provide
for us magnificent burial, my kin.

Cold hills already lie
staring down at our cornfields covetously.[15]

By the end of the year Cowley seemed comfortably settled in Montpellier. He was pleased to have time for full pursuit of his literary interests, and he was surprised to discover that New York magazine editors were not interested in material by Americans written in America. All of Kenneth Burke's most recent short stories, for example, had been rejected. But from France, Cowley was publishing everything he wrote and sent back home. He wrote to Burke, "Stories seem surprisingly easy to sell from here. It is the duty of any writer who wishes to sell himself to this age to travel three thousand miles away from it." The lesson of this experience led Cowley to assert a principle which, he cynically argued, would hold true beyond the fickle and sometimes ephemeral interests of New York's literary editors: "It is not true that fame never depends upon ability. I am sure that if one searched

15. Malcolm Cowley, "Mountain Valley," rpr. as "Hickory Cove" in *Blue Juniata* (New York, 1929), 16.

far enough back through history, one could find a great man whose reputation rested on what he had done and not on his press agents. Perhaps even Vergil is not entirely a creation of the publishers of textbooks." [16]

But Cowley himself, as a young literary journalist seeking money and reputation, was not about to spurn good fortune when he met it, and New York editors were buying his journalism mailed from France. One long article he published in the November 21 New York *Herald Tribune* reported the unveiling on November 6 of a monument to Rabelais in Montpellier. Like the article on his literary generation, it was well received, with a full-page spread in the *Tribune*'s Sunday pages, and included a photo of the Villeneuve sculpture of Rabelais and illustrations by Cowley's wife. Cowley's article on Rabelais was a good report of the festivities surrounding the event, but it also raised the question Cowley had been discussing with Burke concerning the failure of modern audiences (in America as well as in France) to support and recognize young artists. The article also suggests how his ideas were developing, for it ended with praise of Rabelais' great love of country, common people, and the natural, human world which he had so warmly and richly recorded. The essay is important because it hinted at what would increasingly become the subject of a good deal of Cowley's subsequent criticism: his praise of the humanism and realism of classical and Renaissance art, which was sharply in contrast to the modern aesthetic. Indeed, no writer symbolized that humanism better than Rabelais. [17]

Cowley's situation in southern France provided him a somewhat detached perspective on the activities of his friends, since his time in Paris was limited to short holiday visits when he was free from his class schedule at Montpellier. This view was evident in his reaction to several events during December. Early that month Matthew Josephson notified Cowley that he had arrived

16. Cowley to Burke, December 1, 9, 1921.
17. See Jacques Le Clercq, Introduction to *The Complete Works of Rabelais* (New York, n.d.).

from New York and settled in a cold-water flat in Montmartre. Josephson also described the newest literary sensation of Paris, the Dadaists, and how, with a bit of good fortune and brashness, he had been introduced to the Dadas and accepted into their circle. He also informed Cowley that Gorham B. Munson had read Cowley's essay in the New York *Evening Post* on the new generation of writers and wanted to start a literary magazine to publish their work. What Josephson did not indicate was that Munson wanted his magazine, *Secession* (a title taken from the Austrian art group of a decade earlier known as the Vienna Sezession), to be a vehicle of American avant-garde agitation and art.[18]

Cowley seems to have had no idea of Munson's intention to use the magazine for this purpose and instead looked upon the journal as merely a potential outlet for the work of his artist friends. Indeed, much of his time during the remainder of December was spent arranging a group of poems which he sent back to Foster Damon in Boston for inclusion in a book titled *Eight More Harvard Poets*, which was published several months later under Damon's supervision. The book was meant to represent the poetry of the Harvard men in the classes after Eliot and Aiken, those of the war years.[19]

The Cowleys spent Christmas of 1921 in Montpellier with several new French friends and the Stewart Mitchells from Harvard. The autumn, Cowley wrote at the end of the year, had been thoroughly satisfactory. His free-lance writing and translating had earned some money, he had had time to think and write seriously, and he had become convinced from brief trips to Dijon and Marseille that his situation was perfect. He loved the quiet of the small city university and the provincial ambience, where "one could be natural" and "no affectation was needed."[20]

By early January of 1922, Cowley was writing more frequently

18. Josephson to Cowley, December 6, 1921.

19. Cowley to Burke, December 9, 1921; Damon to Cowley, October 18, 1921.

20. Cowley to Burke, December 23, 1921.

to several friends as he began to take notice once more of the increasing effect of avant-garde aesthetics. For example, the first three issues of the new magazine *Broom* were dominated by the work of the European moderns, including Picasso, Jacques Lipschitz, Juan Gris, and André Derain and Americans such as Man Ray. The first issue began with a manifesto declaring its intention to bring to American audiences the best contemporary art in Europe and to sweep away the traditional art of the past: "Throughout, The Unknown, Path-Breaking Artist Will Have . . . . At Least An Equal Chance With The Artist of Acknowledged Reputation." A short story by James Oppenheim dramatized the "Freudian" idea of escape from the scientific culture of repression which characterized the modern age. And the issue concluded with a long essay by Emmy Veronica Sanders attacking the "materialist monster" of America.[21]

The second issue contained a speech by Joseph Stella, an avant-garde New York painter, to a league of artists in the city. The speech indicated the degree to which the tenets of modern aesthetic discourse had been adopted by American artists: "The modern painter knowing that his language deals with form and color proclaims all the purity of his own language and repudiates the assistance of all those red-cross societies which camouflage themselves: literature, philosophy, politics, religion, ethics." Stella concluded with a typical appeal for "modern" artists to continue the quest for psychic exploration of the unknown and to reject the past traditions of art.[22]

Cowley was observing all this, including the increase of radical aesthetic ideas in America in journals like the *Dial* as well as *Broom*. A poem he sent to *Broom*, which was printed in the third issue of the magazine (January, 1922), demonstrated his at least partial sympathy with the modern literary trend. Apparently based on his recent reading of Proust, the poem juxtaposed scenes of a once elegant château (and the decadent behavior of characters

21. *Broom*, I (November, 1921).
22. Joseph Stella, "On Painting," *Broom*, I (December, 1921), 122.

seemingly drawn from Proust's nineteenth-century aristocratic
society) against the gutted reality of the modern world, the old
having been destroyed by the events of World War I. The satire of
the poem was directed less at the war than at the pretensions of
the old order.

Jean tells me that the Senator
came here to see his mistresses,
and having passed the gilded door,
was ushered regally—Jean says—
past genuine Flemish tapestries,
velvets and mahoganies,
to where the odalisque was set,
the temporary queen, Odette.

. . . An eighteenth-century château
rebuilt to meet his lavish taste,
painted and gilt fortissimo;
the Germans, grown satirical,
had hidden a machine-gun nest
underneath the banquet hall.

The trenches run diagonally
across the alleys and the lawns,
and jagged wire from tree to tree;
the lake is desolate of swans;
in tortured immobility,
the deities of stone or bronze
await a new catastrophe.

Phantasmagorical at night
yellow and white and amethyst,
the star-shells burn, and Verey lights,
and silent waters of the mist
submerge the landscape, till we feel
like drowned men, tragical, unreal.

And recent ghosts appear: Odette,
in skirt ballooning at the hips
tosses a hasty kiss and slips
away to taunt the Senator

who, strong with marc and anisette,
his red beard waggling in the wind,
pursues her like a matador.

The mist creeps riverward. A fox
barks underneath a blasted tree.
An enemy machine-gun mocks
this ante-bellum comedy
and then falls silent, while a bronze
Silenus, patron of these lawns,
stands riddled like a pepper-box.[23]

Cowley's criticism of Proust's aristocratic society and ideas was
more explicit in several letters he wrote in January, 1922. In a
long letter of January 12, for example, he described a series of
feelings that had recently troubled him, including his fear of
poverty, of being a social outcast, and of hurting people. His
problem was made acute by the nature of literary journalism and
criticism. He also reiterated that the escape to provincial France
could only be temporary and must eventually be resolved by
return to America: "Six months more of New York and I would
have been fifty, but in this calm Protestant town I begin to drop
my factitious years. . . . I am not convinced of the vanity of life
and one should be able to retire to an unwalled garden."[24]

But the bulk of the letter concerned Cowley's reaction to the
seemingly unquestioned adoption of the ideas of modern aesthetics by Burke, Josephson, the editors of *Broom*, the *Dial*, and
scores of other American artists: "Lastly I have begun to make
some observations on Contemporary Aesthetics. I wish to hold
the ideas of others and ourselves up to a mild ridicule; for
example, the fashion in which Art is taking the place of Religion—the desire that the artist should be poor and chaste. The
fear of Being Understood, which I wish to tie up with Rosicrucianism. The Search for Originality, and all these other ridiculous

23. "Château de Soupir: 1917," *Blue Juniata*, 63–64.
24. Cowley to Burke, January 12, 1922.

ambitions of our times." His studies at Montpellier had made him aware of another theory of literature, that of classical France, particularly the ideas of the seventeenth-century French writer Nicolas Boileau and the classic French theater: "[Boileau] was the theorician [*sic*] of the group of Molière, La Fontaine, and Racine. Their practice has survived where much of his theory has died; nevertheless he was alive enough so that the first two pages of The Ars Poetique would make a telling criticism of let-us-say-D. H. Lawrence. His watchwords were Truth, Nature, Good Sense. We are changing all those watchwords, but we have to think carefully before denying them, and Boileau makes one think." [25]

This interest in classicism, particularly the drama, and in the aesthetic values of French classical writers, was important for Cowley and began to counterbalance the avant-garde ideas being propagated in contemporary France. Boileau's aesthetic had been a central element in the philosophy of the Enlightenment and provided an insight into its beliefs about the relationship of art to society, history, and human reality, as described by Ernst Cassirer:

Boileau had been recognized as the "law-giver of Parnassus." His work seemed finally to elevate aesthetics to the rank of an exact science in that it introduced in the place of merely abstract postulates concrete application and special investigation. The parallelism of the arts and sciences, which is one of the fundamental theses of French classicism, now appeared to have been tested and verified in fact. Even prior to Boileau this parallelism had been explained on the grounds of the common derivation of the arts and sciences from the absolutely homogeneous and sovereign power of "reason." [26]

It was the rational basis of classical aesthetics that attracted Cowley.

Study of classical French literature preoccupied Cowley through the end of January. He had recently seen a local produc-

25. *Ibid.*
26. Ernst Cassirer, *The Philosophy of the Enlightenment* (Princeton, 1951), 280.

tion of *Tartuffe*. In late January he also met Alfred Kreymborg, the coeditor of *Broom*, who was buying poems from Cowley that were decidedly not avant-garde in style. Cowley found he liked Kreymborg because of his openness to different types of art. In addition, the *Dial* editors in New York continued sending him books for review. One review he completed in late January, of a book of translated classical Chinese poetry done into English by Amy Lowell, showed that his interest in classicism was increasing. The effect of all this study was evident in several letters written at the end of the month:

Really that book of Chinese poems produced a tremendous effect on me. Obviously classicism means clarity, honesty, and . . . freshness, and obviously these Chinese poems possess these qualities to the highest degree.

Do you know I was always rather ashamed of myself because I wasn't sufficiently unintelligible. Now I see that the most ridiculous feature of modern writing is the fear of being understood. We wish to be the priests each of our own little sect, and each sect has its rosicrucian secrets only to be revealed to the proselyte who has passed through the seven stages of the novitiate. Meanwhile the proselytes are too busy founding little sects of their own. And literature remains the art of conveying ideas and shows no disposition to adopt either Dada or Rosicrucianism.

I want instead to reduce everything to its simplest terms, and to build up subtlety by the opposition of simple statements.[27]

In a letter written January 28, 1922, Cowley returned to the subject: "I feel more than ever the need of intelligent society. Not being a romantic I have no wish for magnificent solitude. I want to write comedies and satires, and comedies and satires require an audience." He had recently read "Gerontion," and now to Burke he angrily associated it with the trend of contemporary art he called "Rosicrucian," named after a nineteenth-century French Symbolist group: "Mr. T. S. Eliot named one of his pieces Geron-

27. Cowley to Burke, January 23, 1922.

tion; I never understood what he meant by it until I examined my Larousse. 'Geronte: (du gr. *Geron*, viellard), nom habituel du père or du personnage grave de la pièce de notre ancienne comedie. . . . ' If Mr. Eliot had named his poem 'Pantaloon' he would have carried the same meaning to several times as many people; he preferred to be rosicrucian, and I have no wish to be. I want an audience." [28]

One wonders how many contemporary readers would have understood either title. Communicability in art was becoming one of Cowley's fundamental tenets. Indeed, his association of Eliot with the Symbolists and his dislike of their aesthetic were understandable, considering his predilection for representation of nature in art and for clarity of expression. The aesthetic of the "Salon de la Rose + Croix," or the revival of fifteenth-century Rosicrucianism, had been announced in the 1880s by an artist who called himself Sâr Péladan for "mysterious" effect:

The Salon de la Rose + Croix wants to *ruin realism*, reform Latin taste and create a school of idealist art. . . . For greater clarity, here are the rejected subjects, no matter how well executed, even if perfectly: History painting. . . . Patriotic and military painting, such as by Meissonier, Neuville, Detaille; All representations of contemporary, private or public life. . . . All rustic scenes; All landscapes, except those composed in the manner of Poussin. . . . Architecture: since this art was killed in 1789, only restorations or projects for fairy-tale palaces are acceptable.

The subjects the Rosicrucians would permit included only archaic and esoteric religious doctrines such as "Catholic Dogma from Margharitone to Andrea Sacchi; the interpretation of Oriental theogonies except those of the yellow races." [29]

What Rosicrucianism represented was almost totally alien to

28. Ibid., January 28, 1922.

29. Edward Lucie-Smith, *Symbolist Art* (New York, 1972), 111–12. This quotation abbreviates the manifesto of "The Salon de la Rose + Croix" reprinted in Lucie-Smith's book.

Cowley's developing aesthetic. Its programmatic rejection of anecdotal painting and the subtle repudiation of humanism in art, and all art since the French Revolution for that matter, was an undercurrent that influenced many subsequent modern aesthetic theories. In the same letter describing what Cowley believed to be the Rosicrucian character of modern literature, he described what he felt was the antisocial influence of that literature on the early work of John Dos Passos as evidenced in Dos Passos' recently published war novel *Three Soldiers*, a book Cowley said reminded him of the aesthetic atmosphere at Harvard College:

[I] just read *Three Soldiers*. It is over-written, badly composed. On the other hand it is frank, accurate, splendidly malicious; it introduces half a dozen new characters to literature. I shall never carp against it, for it expresses Dos Passos' generation perfectly and comes too near to expressing our own. I shall never write that kind of novel; I never could. Nevertheless that novel aroused too many memories in me and too many fancies for me to object to it.[30]

The aesthete, or "poet against the world," whom Cowley recognized as the theme of Dos Passos' early work, derived from Dos Passos' Harvard background, which Cowley knew also. This knowledge helped him later become one of the most influential explicators of Dos Passos' work to audiences of the 1930s.

By February Cowley was quarreling with Kenneth Burke, who, back in New York, was still writing short stories "programmed" around formal geometric structures and the psychological theories of Freudian dream analysis. During 1922, he told Burke, New York writers had moved further toward the Rosicrucian. He saw the evidence in their receptivity to the publication of Eliot's *Waste Land*, which was the most glaring example of the trend. The influence of Freud on New York writers and artists was another example. In addition, he cited the cultural "primitive" movement in New York associated with the Harlem Renais-

30. Cowley to Burke, January 28, 1922.

sance as another American expression of the influence of European modernism. Burke appears to have defended many of these modern art currents in letters to Cowley criticizing his defense of "classical" aesthetics. In a letter of late February Cowley replied, explaining that, having just passed his first term exams at Montpellier, he could finally do some thinking about the subject. Amid praise of the smells and sights of early spring in southern France and of the wonderful French cuisine, Cowley again expressed his opposition to the modern aesthetic and its major premise, which he would make famous in *Exile's Return*, that art had become a substitute for religious experience:

Wherefore your two last letters aroused in me a sort of full-bellied tolerance, which of all emotions is the most hateful to you. I mean your indignant attacks on my ridicule of current Aesthetics. . . . You do not partake, except at rare moments, of the Desire to be Misunderstood. You do partake, however, of the substitution of art for religion, which, in spite of your indignant protest, I still consider to be touched with ridicule. But my treatise wasn't in the least aimed at you; it was more an examination of my own mind and a denigration of my own ideas, inasmuch as I had accepted them from other people. Some other evening I am going to explain myself at greater length. . . . I think nothing so beautiful at present as a play by Racine, and if more energetic would write an essay to explain why I think so.[31]

Shortly after this Cowley spent several long meetings walking about the campus and discussing literature with a new faculty friend, Jean Catel, a scholar of American literature who also wrote a column for the *Mercure de France* on the contemporary American literary scene. He later wrote one of the first important works on Walt Whitman, who was already a subject of his scholarship. Catel told Cowley that he had just received a letter from Amy Lowell advising him that Cowley was a "nice boy" but could not write poetry very well and was a better critic. Cowley was hurt by the comment but wrote to Kenneth Burke that he would

31. *Ibid.*, February 27, 1922.

not retaliate in the review of her book on Chinese poetry, which he was to do for the *Dial*. He took her criticism as instruction, and besides he liked her Chinese translations. He admitted that he might not be a very good poet and that "for every hour on a poem I have spent at least ten on criticism."[32]

In a note to the letter appended a week later he summarized again his quarrel with Burke over the assumptions of avant-garde aesthetics:

Tonight I am pretty nearly incapable of thinking, so I cannot make answer to your theories. Except this: both terms of any antinome [*sic*] tend to become of equal importance. Thus Good-Evil; as soon as one has admitted the existence of evil, one is led inevitably to a dualism and a balance. Form-matter is the same kind of antinome [*sic*]. As soon as one has admitted the existence of matter—the independent existence thereof—it becomes just as important as form. The only way to make it less important is to resolve it entirely into smaller forms, thus building what one might call a Berkleyan aesthetic. The other solution is to deny the existence of form: an aesthetic which might be called Neo-Realist or Dreiserian. Both these solutions are logical; neither is sensible. There remain the two illogical solutions. The one is the Dualism of Form and Matter; in this, as I said, both terms, despite one's efforts, tend to become equally important. The final solution is to split up the antinomy into several terms; in other words to erect a pluralistic aesthetic.

Form especially can be so divided. Thus, when we speak of the *form* of a poem, we mean one or all of the following:

1. Its *architectural* form (it is in this sense that we generally employ the term; rather let us say its *geometrical* form.)
2. Its *motion*.
3. Its *rhythm*.
4. Its clarity or lack of it; in other words its expression. (Sentence-structure, etc.)

Now if you proclaim that the geometrical form of a work of art is its most important feature, or if you proclaim that it should be judged by its motion, you are proclaiming something. But if you say that form is

32. *Ibid.*, March 5, 1922.

more important than matter, you are adding only an individual affirmation to a dispute that has lasted since Plato.[33]

Though not immediately recognizable in its substance, or published in any of Cowley's later works, the argument between the two friends helped shape Burke's thinking in the section of his book *Counter-Statement* which he titled "Lexicon Rhetoricae," in which he discussed an issue that riddled twentieth-century critical debate for decades.[34] Cowley was already rejecting the dilemma. His analysis of the issue, though, was characteristic of his developing critical self-assurance in aesthetics. His choice of a critical pluralism in art permitted him to continue his eclectic reading habits and his historical and social approach to literature, which dealt with the ideas and values of art as well as the purely aesthetic context.

By the end of March, 1922, his interest in the practical side of literary life was reinforced. He needed money and admitted that literary journalism, some of which he did as "hack work," was necessary. For journalism at its best, he wrote, the classical discipline was the best training for a writer: "It is the classical brain which builds a perfectly proportioned edifice, which writes prose that is simple and clear, and poetry studiously incorrect."[35]

The disciplined prose of a clearheaded writer was the subject of an essay he began in late March and worked hard on during the first weeks of April. He mailed the essay to New York in an attempt to sell it to Van Wyck Brooks, then editor of the *Freeman*. It is notable that Cowley was thinking increasingly of Brooks, since by 1922 the *Freeman*, with Brooks in the lead, was waging an unsuccessful campaign against the aestheticist tide in contemporary art circles.[36]

33. Note, March 13, 1922, appended to *ibid.*
34. Kenneth Burke, *Counter-Statement* (1931; rpr. Berkeley, 1968), 124–26.
35. Cowley to Burke, March 30, 1922.
36. Susan J. Turner, *A History of The Freeman* (New York, 1963), 95.

The article, which Cowley titled "A Brief History of Bohemia," was published in July. It represented an important statement on the sociology of modern art. He spent ten days working on the piece, and much of its emotional force clearly reflected his experience in Greenwich Village. The irregularity, incoherence, and squalor of bohemian society were, he seems to have thought, also reflected in art and aesthetics. Classical art valued clarity in thinking and living, as well as in aesthetic form. Its highest sense of beauty was "elegance," "an integral quality and not an external quality superimposed on a work of art. It means: proportion, economy of means, rhythm—in short, perfection of the work of art as judged by the standards it sets itself." [37]

Nothing was more contrary to this idea of elegance of thought, design, and living than the modern avant-garde artistic bohemia. Cowley's essay traced the historical rise of the bohemian artist in nineteenth-century France and described a recent ceremony held in the Luxembourg gardens in Paris by a group of Frenchmen honoring a bust of Henry Murger, the author of *Scènes de la vie de Bohème*. Cowley sarcastically noted that no one from the contemporary café society of Paris showed up, nor did any of the bourgeoisie, a point he emphasized to distinguish the bohemia that had housed writers in the past and the contemporary vulgarized commercial version. He reviewed the content of Murger's book and asserted that Murger had succeeded only in "vulgarizing the conception" of artistic bohemia and had romanticized a historical reality that had been dangerous to artists. The history of the real early bohemians, Gautier, Nerval, and Musset, illustrated this danger. The essay concluded with a blistering attack on the entire mythology of bohemianism and warned of its debilitating influence on modern artists:

[Murger] is largely responsible for an ideal of artistic life which has wasted several generations of talent; an ideal which has peopled more sanitariums, jails, and venereal wards than it has ever filled museums.

37. Cowley to Burke, April 12, 1922.

When he composed "La Vie de Bohème" he was thinking of the adventures of his own friends, but he changed and prettified everything in the writing. . . . Today Bohemia is a vast enterprise which could be capitalized at several millions. Starting as a revolt against the bourgeoisie, it has become as much the property of the bourgeoisie as any other business-venture.[38]

With revisions and the addition of a historical contrast to the concept of a literary Grub Street, this essay became part of the substance of Cowley's chapter "War in Bohemia" in *Exile's Return*; it was sometimes incorrectly interpreted as a product of his "Marxist" politics in the 1930s.

Much of the month of April, 1922, Cowley spent studying, relieved by the knowledge that his scholarship from the American Field Service had been renewed for another year and that six reviews and essays he had written during the early spring were going to be published.[39] When the first issue of the new magazine *Secession*, which Matthew Josephson and Gorham Munson had helped put together, was published in April, Cowley responded critically. His contribution was a poem that opened the issue and was a combination of sections of free verse and prose-poem. Though experimental in structure, it was written in a clear, intelligible manner. With imagery recalling again the solid Pennsylvania landscape of Cowley's youth, it described the impressionistic memories of a young man on a train from New York to Pennsylvania.

> . . . He turned to watch the hills
> weave up and down like rapid, green
>   ungraceful
> dancers against the curtain of his eyes;
> to watch the houses mingle, and his breath
> a moving mist that crept across the pane. . . .

38. Malcolm Cowley, "A Brief History of Bohemia," *Freeman*, July 19, 1922, p. 439.
39. Cowley to Burke, April 13, 1922.

Oblongs of light reflected from the train
gleamed along the mountainside and vanished;
a whistle drifted eastward with the wind.

He buttoned his coat, marched off into the
          darkness,
which step by step preceded him, until
he seized and wrapped it three times
          round his shoulders;

bending his shoulders under the weight of
          darkness,
he stumbled on with his burden of stars
          and hills.[40]

The rest of the issue, however, showed how thoroughly Munson and Josephson had been caught up in the spirit of the avant-garde. Josephson translated and printed several works of his new Paris Dada friends, such as Louis Aragon and Tristan Tzara, and he wrote an essay tracing their lineage to Rimbaud and Lautréamont. Josephson's essay discussed the work of André Breton and Paul Eluard, as well as that of Aragon and Tristan Tzara, and described their behavior not as the high jinks of "exhausted and disenchanted young men" but the behavior of talented, fun-loving avant-gardists.[41]

Gorham Munson's contributions included a long essay on the linguistic experiments and aesthetic revolution of Dadaist literature. The essay was somewhat contradictory, on the one hand challenging the Dadaist assumption that literature could be abstract without specific referential or descriptive solidity; on the other describing Tristan Tzara's aesthetic as "a sign esthetic. His poetry is a challenge to further research in the esthetic nature of words." But what most disturbed Cowley about the issue was

40. Malcolm Cowley, "Day Coach," *Secession*, I (Spring, 1922).
41. Matthew Josephson [Will Bray], "Appollinaire: Or Let Us Be Troubadours," *Secession*, I (Spring, 1922), 9–13.

that Munson closed his essay with a statement that *Secession* had originated with Cowley's essay on a new generation of writers, leaving the impression that Cowley was in accord with the editorial views of the new magazine. And that editorial position was one of avant-garde polemics, typical of the tendency of the little magazines of the era to fire fusillades at rival journals. In a closing essay Munson blasted the *Dial* in New York for its lack of aesthetic taste, consistency, or point of view. He ridiculed a recent *Dial* prize to the older realist writer Sherwood Anderson and called the *Dial*'s tastes a "vulgarization" of its legitimate business to publish the work of new artists.[42]

The very title of the journal indicated it was "seceding" from the mainstream culture of America, and Cowley reacted privately with caution hoping it would improve. He wrote Kenneth Burke on April 13, 1922, that Josephson and Munson's literary politics were dominating the journal and that they often feuded with each other and tended to be immature in editorial judgment. The first issue, he believed, was "disappointing" in its quality and positions, but at a total printing cost of twenty-five dollars and a small audience, the men should use the magazine to publish works that could not get placed elsewhere.

In a letter to John Brooks Wheelwright, however, Cowley expressed considerable anger about the Dadaist content of the issue, particularly a long piece of prose rambling by Josephson called "Peripatetics." Wheelwright was working on the journal from Boston and New York, and he was a friend of Munson's. He was also a Harvard dropout, poet, and close friend of Foster Damon's. In making final editorial corrections of the book *Eight More Harvard Poets*, he had written Cowley for comments on that volume and on *Secession*. In a long letter written in late April, 1922, Cowley gave his fullest reaction to the Dada infatuation of his friends. The ideas in this letter were to become a standard theory of later

42. Gorham Munson, "A Bow to the Adventurous," *Secession*, I (Spring, 1922), 15–19; Munson, "Exposé No. 1," *ibid.*, 22–24.

academic criticism, and Edmund Wilson argued the same theory in the first chapter of *Axel's Castle* a decade later. Cowley wrote:

I am convinced that another age will speak of ours as the logical unfolding of the romantic movement . . . romanticism carried to the limit of formlessness, immediacy and unintelligibility.

But everything I have said is utterly valueless without a definition of Romanticism. I mean by it the idea that matter is more important than form, the emotions than the intellect, and complex and inexpressible concepts more than clear concepts . . . mystical nationalism demands the slavery of the intellect; Freudianism is greeted as a final victory over conscious thought.

But I wander among grandiose ideas which are the opposite of the sober clarity I demand. I have a very shallow foundation for theories on [*sic*] society; among literary ideas I feel more certain. Let us demand a literature which preserves the virtues of classicism without its vices, a literature, in other words, which still possesses the sentiment of nature, which remains emotional and imaginative, but in which the emotions and the imagination are not given free license. A literature which may strive for complex effects, but which gains them with sentences and paragraphs which are absolutely lucid. An architectural literature from which is disengaged an impression of proportion as from a fine building. A literature, finally, which is a literature and not a theft from life (of it one will never repeat the judgement: That's a fine novel; I know a man just like the hero).

I think we are all fools if we don't work and if we don't work together. The requisite for an intelligent literature (as distinguished from an emotional literature) is an intelligent society, and an intelligent society may consist of only half a dozen people. It would be a mistake to found a school; that would mean that these half dozen men had only one idea. Many ideas can be born and be polished by rubbing against each other.

American literature suffers just now from a lack of such ideas. One can reduce Harold Stearns to one syllogism—Puritanism is bad, America is puritan—American is bad. . . . Mencken has perhaps two or three other ideas; Van Wyck Brooks may reach the complexity of six or seven. But most of our novelists have not even one (and someone said that Wilson had a single-track mind!)

And yet America is not, like England, incongenial to ideas. It is a land of sunlight and clear forms—no fogs—and it welcomes clear ideas when it finds them. I think the laziness of our unintelligenzia [*sic*] is borrowed from a too-close reading of the London *Nation*.

Therefore, let us work for the clear play of ideas. We need a magazine. . . . We need a theatre. . . . We need a Maecenas.[43]

A notable point of this letter is Cowley's apparent defensiveness about American culture. His literary patriotism and hopefulness about the possibilities for American culture differentiated him from many of his contemporaries, and his allusions to such older influential cultural critics of the time as Mencken and Stearns indicated his awareness of their writings on the "failure" and "barbarism" of America's "puritan" culture, theses expounded in works like Mencken's essays in the *Smart Set* or his "National Letters" and in books like Brooks's *America's Coming-of-Age*.[44] Mencken's attribution to democracy of an inherently tasteless and uncultivated culture particularly rankled Cowley, and he wrote about Mencken in later years with a hostility first developed in the early 1920s.

Cowley's defensive literary nationalism was also evident in an essay that was published in early May in the *Literary Review* of the New York *Evening Post*. The article described French reaction to the new American poetry of the prewar years, the poetry of such "naturalists" as Edwin Arlington Robinson, Robert Frost, and Amy Lowell. He noted that in 1914 French students of American culture had ignored the work of contemporary American poets but that a recent article in *La Criée* had energetically praised the "American" qualities of several new artists. Cowley gave a long quotation from this essay, which reflected his own values and demonstrated, he said, the need for Americans to recognize that after the war America stood in a new position of cultural, as well

43. Cowley to John Brooks Wheelwright, April 21, 1922.
44. Alstair Cooke (ed.), *The Vintage Mencken* (New York, 1922), 85–106; Claire Sprague (ed.), *Van Wyck Brooks: The Early Years* (New York, 1968).

as political, leadership. This situation required a reevaluation of the American cultural heritage such as some French analysts were carrying on. His citation of a French critic stood as his own personal statement of the need for cultural diversity, artistic pluralism, and appreciation of the rich qualities of American art:

[American poetry] is not limited to a single form: [it demonstrates] a lyricism which combines the acquisitions of English romanticism and French symbolism; a realism utilizing the incomparable possibilities of a language which has been enriched by purely American forms. . . . But if one is seeking something else in poetry, an interpretation in human terms of an imperious reality; a form that is both free and severe; a soul whose fine sincerity expresses itself upon us—then, even if we are ignorant of the civilization which nourishes and impregnates it, we must greet without reserve this splendid adventure which the poets of the New World are furnishing under our eyes.[45]

His review of Amy Lowell's renderings of classical Chinese poems, which had impressed him in January, appeared in the May, 1922, *Dial*. In it he again expounded his ideas on American poetry and modern art. He criticized once again the experimental method of modern literature and the lack of conscious discipline and tradition in contemporary writing:

[Classical Chinese is] a literature that could exercise a beneficent influence on our own. It proves for example—and this contrary to the doctrine of our romantic Freudians—that a great poetry can exist by other virtues than its sexual interest. It offers a resolution of our too-favorite antinome between romanticism and classicism, for it is a literature both universal and concrete, both human and humanistic; a literature that is classical without being mummified. American poetry could learn this from Chinese.[46]

45. Malcolm Cowley, "The French and Our New Party," New York *Evening Post Literary Review*, May 6, 1922, p. 641.

46. Malcolm Cowley, "Bonded Translation," *Dial*, LXXII (May, 1922), 517–21.

His interest in humanistic art was indicated in a poem he published in the May issue of *Broom*. The imagery once more described rural America:

I watched the agony of a mountain farm,
a gangrenous decay:
the farm died with the pines that sheltered
           it;
the farm died when the woodshed rotted away.

It died to the beat of a loose board on the
           barn
that flapped in the wind all night;
nobody came to drive a nail in it.
The farm died in a broken window-light,

a broken pane upstairs in the guest bedroom,
through which the autumn rain
beat down all night upon the Turkey carpet;
nobody thought to putty in a pane.

Nobody nailed another slat on the corncrib;
nobody mowed the hay;
nobody came to mend the rusty fences.
The farm died when the two boys went away,

or maybe lived till the old man was buried,
but after it was dead I loved it more,
though poison sumac grew in the empty
           pastures,
though ridgepoles fell, and though
           November winds
came all night whistling through an open
           door.[47]

    The literary quarrels of brash young writers which Cowley was later to describe satirically in *Exile's Return* were partially related to his own resistance to modernism. In a letter of May 2, 1922,

47. Malcolm Cowley, "Mountain Farm," *Broom*, II (May, 1922), 134.

Matthew Josephson had ridiculed Cowley's "provinciality" as evidenced by his "Farm" poetry, and thought Cowley's defense of classicism, at a time of modern ferment, was pretentious. Josephson was a feisty young writer at the time and appears to have been carried away with youthful exuberance and enthusiasm for his Dada friends and their literary doctrines. His own Dadaism was both innocent and high-spirited. He seemed ignorant of the philosophical implications of Dada doctrines or their latent pessimism. But in the first issue of *Secession* his defense of his Paris friends had included an attack on artistic realism, in which he called Dadaistic subjectivism a rich source of art: "[Dada has] demonstrated that although nature had always been painted as a static landscape in literature it could be rendered in subjective motion or in any of a thousand states."[48] Cowley's defense of classicism, which Josephson had been shown by Kenneth Burke, and his critical defense of literary realism, Josephson thought, were symptomatic of the insensitive and reactionary opinions of the New York literary establishment. He ended his letter to Cowley by declaring Dadaistically that advertising was a better method of literary criticism than vulgarization by discursive analysis.[49]

Cowley responded to the criticism by his friends with restraint and conviction. Kenneth Burke had apparently joined Josephson by calling Cowley's article on Bohemia simple. Two letters in May, 1922, gave Cowley's reaction. He objected to Josephson's denigration of literary criticism. He also admitted that his own "exile" from America could not be permanent and that he must return to fulfill his literary career and face the cultural conditions that had caused him to leave in the first place. The task for Cowley was to find a place to live in America that would be congenial and still provide an income. That meant a country home near America's major literary market, for, he wrote Burke, "I agree

48. *Cf.* Josephson, "Apollinaire."
49. Josephson to Cowley, May 2, 1922.

with you that the ideal life for an American writer is somewhere within two hours of New York." In another letter he said, "I miss the open country and American trout streams." He also defended again his personal literary tastes and convictions:

My talent is not cosmopolitan, and I have no desire to spend my life in France. On the other hand, this existence in the French provinces—like that in the Argentine or a Chinese river town—gives an excellent perspective on America, and under its influence my ideas seem to be clarifying.

Another mention of clarity. I should not be so proud of it if it came without effort. For example this Murger article. It was unjust for you to say that my subject matter was not very complicated at most; it took me ten days to decomplicate my subject matter.

At the close of his letter Cowley admitted to Burke that he had developed a good craftsman's ability to write but still lacked the sophistication, knowledge, and maturity to work on important subjects.[50]

By late May he had also completed a satiric essay on the dilemmas facing young writers forced to find their way in the chaos of all the radical new European aesthetic systems, from Russian Constructivism to Dadaist cerebralism. He sold it to *Broom* and in the process was introduced to Harold Loeb, the owner of the magazine. Cowley learned that Alfred Kreymborg had left the magazine and that Loeb had taken full editorial control. His friendship with a man he first described as "interested in ideas" but buffeted by the competing forces of modern art groups would lead Cowley during the next months to assume increasing responsibility in the direction of the magazine. It also led to his even more direct encounter with the European modernist movement in the arts.[51]

50. Cowley to Burke, May 8, 20, 1922.
51. *Ibid.*, May 20, 1922.

CHAPTER 5

Modernism and Cowley's Development as a Literary Humanist

Early in June, 1922, Cowley began a summer vacation that gave him several months to explore Europe and encounter the ferment of avant-garde art groups in Paris and Berlin. Before leaving Montpellier he had reviewed a critical biography of the Restoration dramatist William Wycherley, written by the French scholar Charles Perromat. He sent the review, unsolicited, to Van Wyck Brooks, then literary editor of the *Freeman*, and Brooks accepted it for his issue of June 7. Shortly before it appeared, Cowley had written Burke: "For three months I have done no thinking on aesthetics. My last difficulty was this: despite the statement that art is creation and not representation, I find that I still judge works of art by their truth-to-life and I don't know whether to change my theory or my practice."[1]

The Wycherley review revealed how strongly Cowley was moving toward a classical aesthetic: "The comedy of the Restoration was perhaps as faithful a reproduction of actual manners as the English stage has ever seen. Its dramatists had a code of morals which included one virtue only, honesty, and by this quality they asked to be judged. . . . Wycherley was even a moralist, if his morality was not exactly that of a Bunyan. He was a moralist with the ill fortune to be judged by other moralities than his own."[2]

Cowley praised the book for situating the playwright in a his-

1. Cowley to Burke, June 2, 1922.
2. Malcolm Cowley, "In Vindication of Mr. Horner," *Freeman*, June 7, 1922, pp. 308–309.

torical context; its readers could sense, he said, that Wycherley had written for a definite theater audience and not for students in college classrooms. He also lauded Perromat for relating the Restoration drama to that of France in the days of Molière and for demonstrating how the ethical standards of the time affected the style and content of its literature. The critical perspective of which Cowley spoke admiringly can best be described as historical, and this was a position he would continue to clarify for himself over the next few years.

Beginning early in June he spent several weeks in Paris. There, through Matthew Josephson, he met several members of the Dada group that surrounded the magazine *Littérature*. He liked Tristan Tzara, then at odds with the group, and saw him frequently. Other new acquaintances were Philippe Soupault, André Breton, about whom he had mixed feelings, and Louis Aragon, whose brilliance impressed him. His personal response to many of these very young avant-garde writers often conflicted with his negative response to their doctrines. At about the same time he was meeting a number of more established French writers, but how he met them is a complicated story that begins with a conversation outside the Café du Dôme.

The conversation was with Ivan Opfer, a feckless Danish artist whom he had known in the Village. Opfer had a bold talent for catching facial expressions, though he always had trouble with his subjects' hands. He had come to Paris with a commission from the monthly *Bookman* to do full-page portraits of leading French writers. He invited Cowley to come along with him and ask the writers questions (in French, which he had not mastered) while he drew their heads; then Cowley could write an article to accompany each drawing. Of course there was no commission for such articles, but Opfer was sure the *Bookman* would accept them. Cowley agreed to take the risk.

They first tried to see Anatole France, but he was in ill health and would no longer admit visitors to his château. Next they approached Henri Barbusse, the author of *Under Fire*, who consented to receive them at his country house. Cowley liked Barbusse immediately and took notes on everything he said, while Opfer did one drawing after another.[3] The article went off to the *Bookman*, which not only accepted it but gave Cowley a commission to write about the other French authors whose portraits Opfer planned to draw. That kept him busy during July, though he did not write the articles till later; he simply visited the authors and took copious notes. Eventually there would be seven articles, published over a period of more than two years.

Among the seven authors interviewed, André Salmon was the least famous but the one with whom Cowley established closest relations. Salmon was a poet of some distinction, who, before the war, had lived with a group of artists and poets who became the founding fathers of modernism. In an unusual gesture he took Cowley aside and gave him a personal account of Paris movements in modernist art and literature since Picasso and Apollinaire had inspired them early in the century. Cowley's education from Salmon about the international flavor of the art scene gave him an appreciation of what Paris might mean to artists. It was, he wrote, a city that did not so much inspire artists as provide congenial conditions in which to work: "Paris has rarely or never produced great literature. There are exceptions: Baudelaire, Verlaine, but the rule is pretty safe. However, Paris has been the condition of great literature."[4]

Late in July the Cowleys had to leave Paris for want of funds. They went to Brussels, where they were lodged and fed by a wealthy uncle of Malcolm's. They overstayed their welcome while waiting for a check from the *Dial*, but finally the check arrived and they were able to continue their travels—first to Munich and then to Imst, a town in the Austrian Tyrol that Josephson had recommended because it was picturesque and inexpensive. In the preceding month Cowley had published little of moment. He had

3. Cowley to Burke, July 22, 1922.
4. *Ibid.*, July 2, 1922.

contributed two reviews to American publications, one of a book
on French pronunciation and the other of two collections of poetry by English writers who have since been pretty well forgotten. He had also printed two poems in the second issue of *Secession*, one of which showed that he had not been unaffected by
Modernist ideas. Part of it reads:

And there are melodies that assault the body,
entering in at the mouth, the ears, the nose,
the pores beneath the armpits, and having taken
possession of me utterly, burst through
the parchment armor of skin.[5]

Though it teetered on the edge of parody, the poem was better
than most of the second issue of *Secession* (except for poems by
e. e. cummings and an experimental story by Kenneth Burke). In
general the issue reawakened the quarrels among Cowley's writer
friends. Tristan Tzara had contributed a nonsense story called
"Mr. AA the Anti-Philosopher," translated by Josephson, who
himself contributed a story called "The Oblate" that used experimental techniques to portray the primitive sexual drive beneath
industrial culture. He celebrated an ideal world of intellect opposed to the "hateful reality" of the modern city and mass society.
Finally, in a long essay on the state of literary journalism, Gorham Munson once again thwacked away at the reactionary editorial practices and personalities behind American magazines such
as the *Dial*, the *Little Review*, and *Broom*. He asserted that they
were merely anthologies of dubious taste and wandering principles, whereas *Secession* represented a coherent position.

Munson's essay did not represent Cowley's position, and he reacted by writing a short poem as a parody of what he had been

5. Malcolm Cowley, "Colloquial French," New York *Evening Post Literary
Review*, July 1, 1922, p. 776; Cowley, "Keats and Hearst," *Dial*, LXXIII (July,
1922), 108–11; Cowley, "A Solemn Music," *Blue Juniata* (New York, 1929),
97–98.

reading in *Secession*; it purposely made no sense. Here are the lines in their simple balminess:

Meanwhile I observed him from a gable

to run along the street violently for they were
thirteen and shout like maybe a siren I must tell
Mr Bruce I must tell Mr Robert Bruce I must tell
Mr Robert Bruce by five o'clock for they were
thirteen at table

thus shouting as the clocks tolled five one clock
aping another and he solely human amid the geometry
of houses wailed Too late too late for Babylon is
falling

falling in flat brick walls folding against the
street like painted sets which after the orchestral
triumph of the fourth act come sprawling

I have watched crumbs of brick descend like fragments
of untidy

manna on the tablecloth at which the butler entered
with basketfired japan in an earthenware pot concealed
by a cosy and fishcakes blossoming around it by which
token also I knew that it was Friday alas was Friday[6]

He derisively called the nonpoem "Poem." Without explaining that it was a joke, he sent it to Josephson, who failed to see the joke. Innocently Josephson accepted "Poem" for the next issue of *Secession*, material for which was then being assembled.

Cowley's real attitude toward the Symbolist doctrine of fused sensory perceptions and artistic forms was plainly stated in an August book review of a collection of short stories by Katherine Mansfield. After discussing her individual stories, Cowley ended with a strong defense of the consciously literary and the "rational" distinctions of Mansfield's art. He also reiterated his dislike of the Symbolist doctrine of artistic syncretism.

6. Malcolm Cowley, "Poem," *Secession*, III (August, 1922), 13.

There is no doubt that the stories of Katherine Mansfield are literature. That is, their qualities are literary qualities. . . . They do not dissolve into music, like Mallarmé, or materialize into sculpture like Hérédia. The figures are not plastic; the landscapes are not painted, but described, and they are described usually through the eyes of a character, so that they serve both as a background and as a character study. . . . Her stories are literature because they produce effects which can be easily attained by no other art.

In contrasting her art with Symbolist antididacticism and evasion of realistic depiction, Cowley described Mansfield as a true artist, who, without crudity, nevertheless used literature as a vehicle for statements about human reality: "These stories, at least the fifteen contained in her second volume, have a thesis; namely, that life is a very wonderful spectacle, [however] disagreeable for the actors. Not that she ever states it bluntly in so many words; blunt statement is the opposite of her method." [7]

One sonnet he published in August (though it had been written much earlier) also demonstrated Cowley's idea that the proper subject of art is human reality. Its theme, once again, was the destruction of the American landscape.

They scoured the hill with steel and living brooms
of fire, that nothing living might persist;
here crouch their cabins; here the tipple looms
uncompromising, black against the mist.

All day the wagons lumber past, the wide
squat wheels hub deep, the horses strained and still;
the headlong rain pours down all day to hide
the blackened stumps, the ulcerated hill.

Beauty, perfection, I have loved you fiercely
—even in this windy slum, where fear
drips from the eaves like August rain, and scarcely
a leaf sprouts, and a universe of pain

7. Malcolm Cowley, "The Author of Bliss," review of Mansfield's *The Garden Party and Other Stories*, *Dial*, LXXIII (August, 1922), 230–32.

labors to bear its stillborn fruit—even here
. . . your long white cruel fingers at my brain.[8]

A second poem, this one published in a little Montparnasse magazine, revealed the ambiguity of Cowley's work, the result perhaps of his proximity to the avant-garde. The poem described a scene along the Mediterranean seashore and blended images of his current observations with others from classical times, all of them connected by the unchanging rhythm of the sea. But the poem ended with two stanzas satirically undercutting the serious poetic mood and occasion, as if Cowley's adolescent personality refused to die, kept alive as it was by the ironic temper of modern European art:

This is, if you consult a map,
the sea that washed the shores of Greece,
from which came riding on the spume
Venus Anadyomene,
and other Venuses descend
up to their, in a word, the sea.

It smells much less of salt than sweat.
Give me a salt-sweaty kiss,
Serena, take my hand and wade
into the sea as warm as piss.[9]

Late in August Cowley went to Innsbruck, a short trip from Imst, for his first meeting with Harold Loeb, the publisher of *Broom*. Loeb was traveling north to Berlin, where subsequent issues of the magazine would be printed at an even lower cost than the earlier ones had been in Rome; his companion was Kitty Cannell, a Paris fashion writer. The travelers met in the crowded railway station at Innsbruck, then climbed to an Alpine meadow,

8. Malcolm Cowley, "Coal Town," *North American Review*, CCXVI (August, 1922), 207; collected as "Mine No. 6" in *Blue Juniata*, 9.

9. Malcolm Cowley, "Mediterranean Beach," *Gargoyle*, III (August, 1922), 12, reprinted as "The Beach at Palavas," *Blue Juniata: Collected Poems* (New York, 1968), 60.

where they sauntered and talked all afternoon. The subject was the future of *Broom*. Loeb, who was not a rich man (though his mother was a Guggenheim), had been spending five thousand dollars a year to keep the magazine afloat.[10] That sum had paid editors, printers, and writers and had produced the most influential of the magazines then bringing examples of European modern art to an American audience. Just how should its work be continued?

It was agreed that afternoon that Loeb should continue as the editor of *Broom* as well as its publisher. Matthew Josephson would have charge of the Berlin office as managing or associate editor. Cowley would go back to France as a roving representative; he would find new authors, if he could, and translate their work. Anything of his own that he submitted to *Broom* would be printed. It was an arrangement that delighted Cowley, for it gave him some influence (and a very little money) without responsibility.[11]

When he started back to Imst the railway station was still crowded with *Valutaschweine* or profiteers of the exchange—and was he not one of them? His social conscience was reawakening. Austria, where the depreciated krone sold at seventy-five thousand for the dollar, had been invaded by tourists, exiled European royalty, and a variety of carpetbaggers. The spectacle was disillusioning. Cowley wrote: "I don't see how such a thing as pure literature can come out of Austria for the next ten years."[12]

In September Cowley and his wife took a brief trip to Reutte, just across the German border. After settling Peggy he made an expedition to Vienna, a longer trip during which he dozed through the night on the hard cushions of a second-class train. This time he was on a mission for *Secession*. He had promised Josephson that he would proofread the third issue, and Josephson had given him twenty-five dollars to pay the printer; that was all

10. Cowley to Burke, September 10, 1922.
11. *Ibid.*, August 22, 1922.
12. *Ibid.*, August 20, 1922.

the issue cost. Thus he was acting for the two magazines that had become major voices of American "avant-gardisme" while he himself was opposing the avant-garde.

Loeb had written an essay for the May *Broom* that revealed his own divided attitude toward American culture. In it he described the presence of American artistic "exiles" in Europe as their response to a capitalist-dominated culture in which artists were destitute while robber barons and bankers were rich, and the general democratic populace was ignorant of all cultural values. Loeb's essay concluded, however, by echoing Van Wyck Brooks in calling for a new effort to unite the highbrow and lowbrow in American culture.[13]

But by the fall of 1922 *Broom* had done little to bridge those cultural divisions. Instead, it had published work from almost every representative avant-garde art movement in Europe and experimental works by almost every individual modern artist, both American and European. Some of those works included reprints of old essays, poems, or manifestos as well as prints of paintings done by Italian Futurists, German Expressionists, Russian Constructivists, and French Dadaists. The influence of several young Americans on Loeb was evident also in the way Matthew Josephson and Gorham Munson were dominating *Broom* during the summer of 1922. For example, the June issue closed with Loeb's greeting to *Secession* as a new publication. And in essays he accepted for the July and August issues he gave Josephson a further opportunity to propagate the Dadaism of his Paris friends. In one essay Josephson had sung the praises of Dada's "irrational poetics" and of its cultural hero Isidore Ducasse: "'The Songs of Maldoror' form a legend on an heroic scale of the naked human passions working out their destinies. . . . With the nullification of human reason, the mind abandons itself to a sort of destructive sincerity, whereby all may be denied or posited, and nothing is impossible."[14]

13. Harold Loeb, "Foreign Exchange," *Broom*, II (May, 1922), 176–81.
14. Matthew Josephson, "After and Beyond Dada," *Broom*, II (July, 1922), 346–50, and "Exordium to Ducasse," *Broom*, III (August, 1922), 3.

This extreme romanticism was also evident in the concerns of a number of Cowley's other friends at the time. Foster Damon was publishing poetry in *Broom* with "strange" and "fabulous" imagery while completing a pioneering book on Blake. *Broom* was serializing Luigi Pirandello's *Six Characters in Search of an Author* as well as Ducasse's blasphemous book *The Lay of Maldoror*, translated by Josephson. Pages of Expressionist painting by Modigliani and Matisse stood next to experimental word arrangements by Wallace Stevens and Gertrude Stein.

Cowley's meeting with Loeb late in August appears to have begun a small shift in *Broom*'s editorial interests. Cowley described Loeb in early September as a confused man, buffeted by the egos and sexual entanglements of the American art colony, a judgment Hemingway made famous in his caricature of Loeb as Robert Cohn in *The Sun Also Rises*. But Cowley also liked Loeb personally and felt he had good instincts while needing to be given self-confidence.[15] Loeb seems to have liked Cowley, too, and years later remembered Cowley's influence on him in that late summer of 1922:

My opinion of Cowley . . . had risen during the years. No one wrote better letters or contributed such consistently good material to *Broom*. . . . Malcolm refused to be hurried. When a question was put to him, the lines between his eyes deepened and the quizzical expression froze. Nothing else happened. Often the silence seemed interminable. But when he finally spoke, his words meant something.

I particularly admired this trait, his waiting until he knew what he wanted to say. . . . I offered Malcolm a position on the magazine— cooperation from a distance by writing, translating, and rounding up other writers who should be appearing in our pages.[16]

For all their differences, the American Dadaists of 1922 had one common trait—an optimistic belief in the potential for American culture. Whatever his infatuation with Dada repre-

---

15. Cowley to Burke, September 10, 1922.

16. The events and several letters between the men are described in Harold Loeb, *The Way It Was* (New York, 1959), 221–25 and 229–30.

sented (and it seems mostly to reveal his immaturity),
Josephson's writings were a defense of American popular culture.
And Loeb published an essay in the September, 1922, *Broom* that
was forceful in stating his optimism for America. The essay described America's "mystical" infatuation with money and business as a kind of religion. American artists' excessive cultural criticism, Loeb argued, was succeeding only in damaging the potential for a cultural renovation of the nation. A too ready adoption
of the "decadent" modern art of Europe was also a danger.
Overall, Loeb urged a reconsideration of the potential of American culture, which he believed was in a stage of "formative-
creative" transition.[17]

The material by European artists that Loeb was given to publish at the time, however, was almost exclusively experimental
forms of modern art. Indeed, the celebration of machinery and
the "aesthetic beauty" of industrial technology, which was a
major theme of both Constructivism and Futurism, was hardly
the best means of capturing middle-class American audiences so
as to build cultural bridges.

Cowley's reaction to Loeb and *Broom* remained mixed. He
found that Loeb respected the clarity of his work and would print
anything he submitted. But Cowley also felt Loeb was not deci-
sive enough to set a clear course for the magazine in accord with
the Americanism Cowley wanted to encourage.[18]

Cowley's strongest reaction to the alignment of his American
writer friends with Dadaism and Constructivism came after he
proofread the third issue of *Secession*, which was dominated by the
work of Josephson and Munson. In "Mr. Blunderbuss" Josephson
attacked several New York literary magazines for criticizing *Secession*'s ideas and for failing to be receptive to new experimental art.
Much of the issue consisted of essays flaunting a bellicose avant-
garde aesthetic philosophy, simplified Freudianism, and the ad-

17. Harold Loeb, "The Mysticism of Money," *Broom*, II (September, 1922),
115–30.
18. Cowley to Burke, September 10, 1922.

vocacy of cultural primitivism, romanticism, and linguistic experiment. The lead story by Waldo Frank attempted a kind of
interior monologue by a lonely man amid the clutter of a modern
city. The man meets a Negro whore in a bar and, with the release
of primitive sexuality which the liaison affords, attains a mystical
freedom and pleasure. The issue also contained translations of
poems and stories by Josephson's Dada friends, including Philippe
Soupault and Hans Arp. Arp's story "Arp the Trapdrummer"
attempted to create the impression of the Dada credo in words, a
confused welter of sounds.[19]

The issue was, in effect, all Josephson and Dada. Cowley's
letters at the time indicate an angry reaction to both the content
of the issue and the manner in which it was being advertised as
the reflection of a group taste. He wrote Kenneth Burke in late
September:

I just blew in from Vienna where I corrected the proof-sheets of *Secession*
3. I swore lustily as I corrected. Kenneth, that number stinks of bad
writing, Dada. . . . The story by Waldo Frank is abominable. The
story by Matty is abominable. The comment is the abomination of
abominations. . . . Possibly the whole number may be suppressed.
Certainly it will be if the postal authorities happen to read that story by
Waldo Frank. Let us hope they do.

For reasons of space I suppressed a four-page open letter to you by
Will Bray [a pseudonym of Josephson's]. It was much more interesting
than Matty's other contributions to the issue, but with your reply it
would even be more interesting. Also he had suggested that I leave it
out if necessary.

Matty speaks of critical prose as hack work. He writes it that way,
without elegance, without logic, with the worst vocabulary of the
newspaper hack. . . . The whole weakness of *Secession* is the fact that it
is supposed to be a group organ and that the group falls apart in the
middle. I often contradict myself but if there's one thing I believe in, it
is good writing. With you I have been trying to work towards solidity
and elegance, towards a to-some-extent classical reaction against the

19. *Secession*, III (August, 1922).

muds and fogs of contemporary literature. . . . I repeat that the third number of Secession has got to be suppressed and that Matty alone cannot edit another number. Otherwise to save ourselves we have got to secede from Secession.[20]

The issue was not suppressed, and it resulted, as Cowley had feared, in his being identified with the ideas of his friends. Yet his association with the young American Dadas was bound to lead to misunderstanding of his literary ideas. Gorham Munson remained in New York during the fall of 1922 and began promoting the *Secession* writers as a collective. In an essay he wrote for a Boston little magazine, *S4N*, he called for America's young writers to begin "an unemotional sloughing off of irrelevant drains on one's energies and a prompt deviation into purely aesthetic concerns." Munson acknowledged that the social concerns of writers such as H. L. Mencken and Van Wyck Brooks were valuable, but he argued that a small group of American writers, such as the men associated with *Secession*, should secede from the contemporary American literary milieu, "which believed that literature was social dynamics and that its social significance was paramount." The essay attracted editorial comment in New York and stimulated a series of essays from Brooks in which he objected to the rise of "coterie" literature in America and Europe dominated by doctrines of "pure" literature rather than by human reality.[21]

Late in September Cowley was privately and publicly revealing how much he differed from Munson. In a letter he wrote on September 27 he indicated once more his dislike of the destructive condition of bohemianism while remembering his hunger and ill health in the streets of New York during 1919: "I know that the unfortunate year 1919 played hell with me. I still haven't digested it." He concluded the letter with a clarification of his aesthetic beliefs: "Art is a function not of the individual but of a

20. Cowley to Burke, September 25, 1922.

21. Gorham Munson, "The Mechanics for a Literary Secession," *S4N* (November, 1922). The essay and Brooks's reaction are discussed in Susan J. Turner, *A History of The Freeman* (New York, 1963), 94–95.

civilization. . . . Art is a civilization defining itself. The critic
believes that art has a history, that art is capable of progress, that
the artist and the public react on each other. If he did not believe
this, he would not be a critic. If art is a definition of civilization,
criticism is a definition of art."[22] Much of Cowley's published
writing during the remainder of his time in France reflected this
conviction, as would his future writing.

An imaginary portrait he gave to Harold Loeb in September
and published in the October *Broom* was particularly revealing. It
satirized an imaginary young artist and the apocalyptic rhetoric of
the quarreling modern art movements. It described the young
artist as in a state of mental collapse after shifting between competing aesthetic theories such as the following: "Determinism
. . . mathematical proportion . . . the arts are not one but
many. . . . Art is a common method of purgation, a spiritual
steaming of the bowels. And each man comes, deposits, passes
on———passes on and then is heard no more. It is a noise made
by an idiot, full of sound and fury, signifying nothing . . . nothing." Cowley portrayed the confused artistic scene confronting
this modern artist by satirizing the aesthetic credos of such men
as the Italian Futurist Marinetti:

If a poet wants to express American life, he has got to live it first. . . .
Our age and nation are extraordinary subjects for literature. New forms,
new movements. An intellectual ferment which puts this period on a
par with that of Marlowe and Drake. . . . I want to jump smack into
the middle of it. I want to be a mechanic and set flywheels rotating
at the touch of a button. I want to write poems that have the vigor of
advertising copy. . . . I want you to join me in founding a new literary
school. It will exist in the Fourth Dimension and will describe the time
factor in motion and measurement.

While briefly stating various ideals, the artist-character uncon-
sciously revealed how avant-garde ideas had affected him: "If I
were a tyrant I'd hang every writer ten years older than myself.
The moderns had elevated originality above all other virtues, and

22. Cowley to Burke, September 27, 1922.

sacrificed ideas to sensation. But you cannot build a literature on individual sensation alone." But the piece ended with the young American writer dazed by yet another turn in his quest to find an aesthetic, this time a vision of "carnal harmony," which led "behind the curtain of the flesh . . . to float across a limitless sea of light," or to the symbolist state of new consciousness beyond rationality.[23]

Cowley's serious essays and reviews of the fall, unlike his satires, demonstrated more straightforwardly his conviction about the need for a social art containing discursive ideas. This conviction was clearly expressed in the first of his portraits of Paris literary luminaries written for John Farrar of the *Bookman*. It discussed Henri Barbusse and his rise to celebrity from the relative obscurity of a forty-year career as a working Paris journalist when he won the Prix Goncourt for *Under Fire*. Barbusse had become an outspoken advocate of left-wing political ideas, a man Cowley described as radicalized by his anger at the old French ruling order that permitted World War I and the slaughter of more than a million French soldiers. In his essay he described Barbusse as a pessimist who had been converted to political activism and an art of social ideas: "By 1919, when he wrote 'Clarté,' Barbusse had come to believe in the possibility of a better world, a possibility that is even now within the grasp of life, and he owed it to his experiences in the trenches." In a revealing summation, Cowley quoted Barbusse's reply to criticism by "formalist" artists, who claimed that Barbusse's novel was merely propaganda and that overt politics in art violated aesthetic purity: "My enemies made it political and not my friends. . . . The sort of literature that exists in a fourth dimension and has no connection with modern life: 'pure literature' as people call it, is dead. But the literature of ideas is always living." [24] It is difficult to miss the way Cowley set up this conclusion to express his own sympathy for an art or

23. Malcolm Cowley, "Young Man with Spectacles," *Broom*, III (October, 1922), 199–203.

24. Malcolm Cowley, "Henri Barbusse," *Bookman*, LVI (October, 1922), 180–82.

literature of social ideas. Barbusse had approved the article in September and in a letter he sent Cowley at the time indicated the extent of their agreement about political art and ideas. Cowley introduced Barbusse to Max Eastman, then the editor of *Hearst's International*. Eastman arranged to get Barbusse published in America, where Barbusse believed Europe's destiny was to be determined, and where he saw, regretfully, none but reactionary political forces.[25]

Barbusse seems to have been the first important writer Cowley met who encouraged his convictions about the social content of art. His meeting had also helped Cowley understand how literary power groups can promote or attack a writer like Barbusse. A letter of October 22 to Kenneth Burke revealed that Cowley had applied his lesson to New York's literary power centers, one of which consisted, he wrote, of such literary critics as Edmund Wilson at *Vanity Fair* and John Farrar of the *Bookman*, magazines with wide impact on American publishing and literature. Another consisted of the Algonquin Hotel writers, whose newspaper columns could "sell" a young writer, a group that included Alexander Woollcott and Heywood Broun.[26]

In early November Cowley returned to Montpellier by way of Berlin, where he spent three weeks and was appalled by the spectacle of Germany in the early Weimar Republic. A poem he wrote in reaction illustrated his disapproval of the economic exploitation and moral corruption he saw, but it was self-critical, too, since the young American writers were also in Europe taking advantage of the cheap living.

Following the dollar, ah, following the
  dollar . . . —where it buys most, there
  is the Fatherland . . .

I dipped my finger in the lake and wrote, *I
shall never return, never, to my strange
land,*

25. Barbusse to Cowley, September 2, 1922.
26. Cowley to Burke, October 22, 1922.

my land where plains are daily stretched, where
    forests burn in business hours daily, where
    yellow nameless rivers run and where
cities stand daily on their heads and wave
    proud legs in the air; [27]

The poem described America, then, as a land of conflicting
forces, which the poet loved yet could not fully accept in its paradoxically rich but destructive reality. The poem's title, "Valuta,"
and its substance also became a section of *Exile's Return*.

He did not stay in Montpellier but instead went north to Giverny, a Norman village where Peggy had rented a little apartment over the blacksmith shop. Cowley's shoestring finances and
the petty feuding of American expatriate writers apparently had
begun to irritate and depress him. His vagrant life and the European artistic and economic unrest were unsettling. Cowley sensed
that the literary feuding and lack of editorial direction of the two
magazines he was associated with meant the certain failure of
both and the loss of any remaining steady outlet for his creative
work. [28]

But Cowley's published writings for November did not reflect
these private concerns. In the November *Dial* he reviewed recent
volumes of poetry by his friend Conrad Aiken and by Carl Sandburg. In the review, "Two American Poets," Cowley tried to
distinguish the individual styles of the two men and discussed
what might be the nature of a "characteristic" American poetry.
After comparing the two poets, he concluded that it was impossible to say a single American school of poetry existed and perhaps it was better that way. If Aiken represented the British strain
of contemporary American verse, and Sandburg the distinctively
rough-hewn folk style, then any attempt to reconcile the strains
was certain to lead to conflict:

Except as a party label there is no American poetry. There is no American poetry in the sense that there is French or Chinese poetry. In other

27. Malcolm Cowley, "Valuta," *Broom*, III (November, 1922), 250–51.
28. Cowley to Burke, November 10, 1922.

words there is no poetry so deeply rooted in our soil and tradition that a foreigner can never fully understand it, and I doubt whether such a poetry is to be desired. In spite of all efforts America is not a point of view, a style, or a mode of thought, but a subject merely: . . . American poets do not exist, but (to witness Sandburg and Aiken) there are capable poets in America.[29]

This essay was notable again for defensiveness about American cultural vitality. Pluralism and diversity in art, he seemed to be arguing, were only natural in a country itself so culturally diverse.

At the end of November, 1922, Cowley was writing an essay on Proust's *A la recherche du temps perdu*, a work he had been reading intermittently for several months. The themes of his essay stand in sharp contrast to those he had been articulating about representationalism in art and clarity of communication. Though the essay was not finished until several weeks later, and was not published until the March, 1923, issue of the *Dial*, he wrote Kenneth Burke on November 27 that he wished it to be printed in a conspicuous place, not simply as a book review, because it represented an important statement of his reaction to modern art. Burke was working at the *Dial* as an assistant to the editor, Gilbert Seldes, and he persuaded Seldes to feature the essay.

Cowley began by describing Proust's novel as a major example of the modern literary mind, a book marked by radical new technical characteristics, including an appearance of chaotic organization, the lack of logical narrative design, and a structure determined by the psychological association of events. Cowley conceded the brilliance of individual sections of the novel. He also warned that readers' conventional expectations of narrative sequence would be disturbed. Yet with an astute insight into the work (which filtered through his obvious antagonism to Proust's style of complex, convoluted syntax), Cowley wrote that Proust had, perhaps in spite of himself, created a work still within the

29. Malcolm Cowley, "Two American Poets," *Dial*, LXXIII (November, 1922), 563–67.

tradition of nineteenth-century historical fiction: "Centuries
never begin or end at the proper date: the seventeenth died in
1715 and the eighteenth prematurely in 1789; what we call the
nineteenth century extends from 1815 to 1914 and is the century
of Marcel Proust. No other novelist has described its latter years
more faithfully. . . . *Remembrance of Things Past* is, accurately, a
historical novel."[30]

He continued by describing Proust as radically different from
the great realistic novelists of the nineteenth century because he
expressed the tortuously alienated and expressive relationship
between modern artists and modern society. He had already privately described Proust to Kenneth Burke in similar fashion:

Proust bathes everything in some luminous mental fluid which does not
alter the facts but makes them stand out by moonlight. He is jeal-
ous. . . . The brain of Proust is a tool which he has fashioned to serve
his egoism. It is the sharpest of tools; nevertheless Proust belongs to an
inferior category of artists; whatever type he belongs to, he is its foremost specimen.

His one novel is not a work of art but a gallery in which the separate
portraits are works of art. You walk around observing them; you do not
begin at the beginning and read through.[31]

In his essay, though, Cowley tempered his statement: "Proust's
method, described in two words, is a creative analysis. He de-
composes his emotion into its most minute details . . . and recre-
ates the whole living emotion in himself." Still, he concluded
with an evaluation of Proust that today must seem extraordinarily
naive and wrongheaded, however honest. Cowley called Proust an
eccentric, when in fact it was Cowley's own literary ideals that
were becoming obsolete:

Observe the life of Proust, so different from the ideal of contemporary
writers. He spent most of it in bed, in an interior room hermetically

30. Malcolm Cowley, "A Monument to Proust," *Dial*, LXXIV (March,
1923), 234–40.
31. Cowley to Burke, November 27, 1922.

sealed to prevent drafts; they say he could feel a breath of air three rooms away, and it would set him coughing. He rarely saw the daylight. . . . His own death was only a process of externalization; he had turned himself inside out like an orange and sucked it dry, or inscribed himself on a monument; his observation, his sensibility, his affections, everything about him that was weak or strong had passed into the created characters of his novel.[32]

This essay, an important early statement of Cowley's reaction to modern writers, became, with revisions for style and added information, the substance of his comments on Proust in the section of *Exile's Return* called "Readings from the Lives of the Saints." And though no historian has pointed it out, the opening paragraphs of Edmund Wilson's essay on Proust in *Axel's Castle* (1931) closely echoed Cowley's phrasing. Nothing illustrated his own dissenting aesthetic taste so clearly as a brief commentary he published simultaneously with the Proust essay in March, 1923, discussing a play by the French writer Raymond Rousel called *Locus Solus* in which Cowley described the central French literary tradition as one of classical elegance and clarity of style.[33]

Cowley expressed his opinion of Harold Stearns, Sinclair Lewis, and Ezra Pound in three poems he published in New York in November, 1923. The poems briefly described the dominant personality traits shown by the men and how these traits were reflected in their writing. The poem about Pound, best of the three, captured the crankiness and "dandyism" of a major modern poet:

Condemned to a red-plush room
    in a middle-class hotel
        in the decay of summer,
here prowls the polylingual,
    refractory, irrepressible
        archenemy of convention—

32. Cowley, "A Monument to Proust."
33. Malcolm Cowley, "Comment," *Broom*, IV (March, 1923), 281–83.

red fox-muzzle beard, red dressing gown—
    and growls at his guest while affably
        scratching himself.
"London," he ruminates, "New York,
    can't thinkably live in 'em.
        Provence might do.
When I was in villeggiatura . . ."
The afternoon droops like a hot candle.
    Sweat beads on spectacles
        slither like melted tallow.
Only, from the couch where he sprawls back,
    indomitable that obelisk of beard
        admonishes the heavens. [34]

When Cowley was finally settled in Giverny, fifty miles from Paris, he traveled no more except to the city. He was tired from his wanderings, and his wife had been ill and needed rest. The charm of his location, the inexpensive living, and access to Paris without having actually to live in the city seemed to dissolve Cowley's dissatisfaction with the literary feuds he and his friends were having. Giverny was famous for its landscape, which had been extensively painted by some of France's most famous Impressionist painters. Cowley, too, loved the calm beauty of its landscape: "Giverney is situated near a long hill running east and west, with little copses and wheatfields. A huddle of stone cottages. A little river bordered with poplars, damp green fields, then finally the Seine. Giverney should be familiar to everybody; it has been painted for the Luxembourg, the Metropolitan, the Autumn Salon, and the Independents; by Cézanne, Monet, T. E. [Butler] and J. Butler and Robert W. Chambers." [35] Monet was still active, painting his great water lily pictures. The real world of nature was Cowley's great aesthetic and spiritual healer, and he responded to Monet and Giverny with satisfaction.

34. Malcolm Cowley, "Ezra Pound," New York *Evening Post Literary Review*, November 14, 1922, p. 351; rpr. *Blue Juniata: Collected Poems*, 59.
35. Cowley to Burke, November 27, 1922.

Trips to Paris and a return visit by Matthew Josephson and his wife in December provided Cowley his closest contact with a number of Paris art figures. While drinking at the Dôme, Cowley was introduced to Ford Madox Ford and reported to Burke that "Ford adores Ezra Pound and believes that everything living in English literature comes, like Pound, from America." In Paris Josephson took Cowley to some of the theatrical scandals his Dada friends were staging. Although Cowley would continue to keep his distance from the Dadas, he found them again, as in the summer, much more attractive than their writings, public posturing, and private quarreling made them appear to outsiders: "They are the most amusing people in Paris."[36]

The American theme of his comments, and of Ford Madox Ford's, too, was evident in two works Josephson and Cowley published at this time. Josephson had continued his Dadaist-Constructivist enthusiasm in a long essay in the November *Broom* that discussed books on American civilization, one by George Santayana, which he praised, and the other, *Civilization in the United States*, the famous symposium on the bleakness of American civilization edited by Harold Stearns, which he sharply criticized as wrongheaded. Josephson took issue with Stearns's conclusion that American culture was a failure in such fine arts as sculpture, painting, and literature. He argued that the word "art" had to be viewed more inclusively in the modern age and that the American cultural genius was really expressed in the machinery, motion pictures, and other forms of popular culture that were the expression of a vibrant people.[37] Unfortunately, his essay wandered off into Dadaist ridicule of "high" art and celebration of advertising posters as the new art of the age. Dada antiart and American advertising were thus linked as the new forms Josephson admired. Josephson's remarks were typical Dadaist assertions.

Cowley's reaction to the Stearns book was published in De-

36. *Ibid.*, December 17, 1922.

37. Matthew Josephson, "The Great American Billposter," *Broom*, III (November, 1922), 304–306.

cember. It took the form of another imaginary portrait, this one called "Young Mr. Elkins." Like his satiric poem on Stearns, it derived some of its humor from his exchanges with Josephson and other Dada friends. But it was a serious criticism of the limited perspective of Stearns and his contributors, and it reflected Cowley's defense of America, on grounds that differed from Josephson's. In addition, Cowley took issue with the New York critic Paul Rosenfeld, whom he quoted at the beginning of the fictional portrait. Rosenfeld had written in one of a series of essays in the *Dial* that American culture provided men of sensitive taste and spiritual sensibility so little hope of nourishment that their only alternative had been to leave America. But in being introduced by his mentor Alfred Stieglitz to "fourteen American moderns" between 1912 and 1920—artists, who, like Stieglitz himself and Marsden Hartley, brought to New York the abstract art and "spirituality" of European modernism—Rosenfeld asserted that he had finally sensed a cultural climate in which he could comfortably live:

Perhaps the new world of new expression of life which should have been reached when the feet first stepped from off the boats on American soil has faintly begun. . . . If to-day men on American land are commencing to come into relationship with one another and with the places in which they dwell, it is through the labor of some dozens of artist hands. Through words, lights, colors, the new world has been reached at last. We have to thank a few people.[38]

It was not only Rosenfeld's views about art that clashed with Cowley's theory that art was an expression of civilization and that artists were as much shaped by their society as they created it. Cowley seems to have been especially irritated by Rosenfeld's antinaturalist aesthetic and his irrationalism, values that reflected the mystical religiosity Rosenfeld had absorbed from his friend Waldo Frank, from European modern art, and from the theory of

38. Paul Rosenfeld, "Epilogue: Port of New York," *Port of New York: Essays on Fourteen American Moderns* (1924; rpr. Urbana, 1961), 295.

American cultural inferiority his friends Van Wyck Brooks and
Randolph Bourne had articulated in the war years. For example,
in his essay on the painter John Marin, Rosenfeld declared that
"visionary" qualities were the source of his art, an art that still
reflected the real world but a real world created "just as it is perceived before the reason steps in." In describing the art of Kenneth Hayes Miller, Rosenfeld attributed its appeal to its dream-
like landscape, "not . . . the dream growing out of reality, but to
the dream erected at the expense of a reality and over a reality left
shoddy."[39]

Cowley began his ridicule of Stearns (not Rosenfeld primarily)
by paraphrasing Rosenfeld's beleaguered statement of isolation:
"Apparently the skyscrapers of lower New York had vanquished.
What could one individual assisted by a few dreamers do against
a civilization." And he summarized Stearns's oversimplifications
in words that echoed the thoughts he had expressed to Kenneth
Burke: "Perhaps it was only to produce young Mr. Elkins that
American Civilization existed. . . . Young Mr. Elkins places an
evident value on his facts and yet he collates them around a simple, almost a childish thesis; a single thesis concerning America
and puritanism."[40] Though he in turn had oversimplified Stearns's
ideas, Cowley's essay reflected his personal and emotional defensiveness about America. With more complex discussion and
revisions, his imaginary portrait served as the basis of his analysis
of the "historical ignorance" of his era's rebellious writers in the
section of *Exile's Return* he called "The French Line Pier, 1921."

When Cowley began the new year 1923 in Giverny, he must
have felt increasingly isolated in his literary tastes and convictions. Indeed, his last months in France must have appeared to
him a bit quixotic. Already in early January his discomfort with
modernist art doctrines was reflected in his writing by an increasing effort to counteract what he perceived as avant-garde tenden-

39. *Ibid.*, 160, 135.
40. Malcolm Cowley, "Young Mr. Elkins," *Broom*, IV (December, 1922),
52–56.

cies all around him. The January issues of both *Broom* and *Secession* were dominated by experimental prose and poetry, some of which, like that of Gertrude Stein, Cowley found almost unreadable. And Cowley's friends Kenneth Burke and Matthew Josephson, and other writers including Hart Crane, Marianne Moore, and Jean Toomer, were breaking all conventions in their poetry and prose. In early January Cowley met another young American writer in Giverny, Robert Coates, whom Gertrude Stein memorialized as the "American with flashing red hair" always standing out in the crowds of Parisian *boulevardiers*.[41] Coates was known at the time as the man who had written the first American Dada novel, *The Eater of Darkness*. Though Cowley and Coates were to become lifelong friends, Cowley found his early writing less than inspiring. A letter he wrote in early January objected to the obscurity of all his friends' work, including Kenneth Burke's stories that lacked plot transitions and switched illogically to scenes connected only by the associational memory of the narrator.[42]

[Robert] Coates has been improved by his year in France. He writes stories without punctuation, but he is beginning not to need this camouflage of modernism; he begins to have ideas. . . . And what is the "modern" note that distinguishes authors of the present "advance guard"? Those terms are so distasteful to me that I can't repeat them without quotes, and yet I possess the current weakness for modernity. And the modern note at present is the substitution of associational for logical thought. Carried to the extremity among the Dadas, the modern note is the substitution of absurdity for logic.[43]

The infatuation of his friends with avant-garde styles only made Cowley more stubborn in defense of his own literary interests and aesthetic ideals: "Since writing Two American Poets I have evidently right-about-faced on the question of the impor-

41. *The Autobiography of Alice B. Toklas*, in Carl Van Vechten (ed.), *Selected Writings of Gertrude Stein* (New York, 1967), 186–87.

42. Burke's story "In Quest of Olympus," *Secession*, IV (January, 1923), 5–18, seems to have particularly upset Cowley.

43. Cowley to Burke, January 6, 1923.

tance of American material. The change is largely psychological. America in the distance begins to loom up as a land of promise, something barbaric and decorative and rich. The form-matter pendulum has taken another stroke, and I begin to believe strongly in the importance of using contemporary material."[44]

That conviction, to remain an advocate for realism in literature, was nowhere more evident than in an essay he wrote for the January *Broom* on an artist of the Latin Quarter who had spent years in America, Jules Pascin. Cowley's critical study of Pascin's art was notable in the issue not only because it was one of the few works written in clear English prose but because it championed artistic realism and American society:

Pascin did not paint the wheels or skyscrapers one might expect of a modern artist; he painted people. He painted them in groups as a rule, but his interest in a group was the individuals which comprised it; in other words he was neither futurist nor unanimist but human. . . . The people he drew, if caricatured, are four-square and three-dimensional. Their implications are social, economic, personal, for into his work Pascin puts all his experience, all his knowledge, and not a circumscribed portion labelled aesthetics. Drawing is not his second or fifth language; it is his only language; he uses it to express everything he has seen, with the result that his portfolio of water-colors forms a whole world and a New World; it is Pascin's America.

Before Walt Whitman America hardly existed; to him we owe the pioneers, the open spaces, in general the poetry of square miles. Bret Harte created California and Twain the Mississippi. . . . America is a conception which must be renewed each morning with the papers. It is not one conception but a million which change daily, which melt daily into one another. . . .

Pascin paints the Irish in Boston and not in the West; Jews in New York and not in Florida; Florida niggers and Mexicans in Texas; everywhere races and professions that are socially declassed, socially unembarrassed; perhaps he finds them the best commentary on a civilization.[45]

44. *Ibid.*
45. Malcolm Cowley, "Pascin's America," *Broom*, IX (January, 1923), 136–37.

This essay was Cowley's most complete statement of his realistic ideals. It indicated, too, his belief in a populist, pluralist American culture. The essay and several other writings of this period present a sharply different picture of Cowley during the 1920s from that presented by certain polemical portraits of him written in later years. The essay (which may have reflected Cowley's beliefs more than Pascin's) addressed a theme that he expressed in several other essays during the winter and spring of 1923: the social role of the artist in creating for a society stories, legends, and a common heritage to humanize the natural world.[46] This statement about the purpose of art was incorporated in the closing chapter of *Exile's Return* in 1934.

Cowley was particularly aroused by an editorial in the January *Secession*, in which Gorham Munson attacked Van Wyck Brooks for demanding that artists work within society. Munson claimed that *Secession* was a magazine for artists who had "seceded from the American literary milieu." Cowley angrily responded to Munson's assertion in reply to a statement Munson had made that the *Secession* writers, both in Paris and New York, had "only to play their cards well . . . to dominate the literary situation in New York." In a letter to Kenneth Burke Cowley denounced the idea that the *Secession* writers constituted an avant-garde movement: "What the hell. Is Secession a Cause, a Movement? Are we going to post the village, advising young writers to 'jump on the Secession bandwagon?' What's all this pink tea stuff?" Presumably the term "pink tea stuff" represented Cowley's opinion of Munson's literary politics. He later wrote that writers should do as much as possible to avoid literary politics because they are only self-defeating.[47]

46. In *A Moveable Feast* Hemingway drew a mixed portrait of Pascin, an artist who "was a very good painter," but was also a bohemian rebel; "Pascin looked more like a Broadway character of the Nineties than the lonely painter that he was, and afterwards, when he had hanged himself, I liked to remember him as he was that night at the Dôme" (*A Moveable Feast* [New York, 1965], 102, 104).

47. See Munson's reply to John Brooks Wheelwright's disavowal of Munson's

By the end of January, 1923, he was even more defensive, made so by the continued attacks some of his friends were making on America. Apparently Kenneth Burke, who had never been to Europe, had repeated the conventional wisdom about the superiority of European culture to America's, a judgment partly based on Burke's extensive reading of modern European writers. Cowley replied that he was tired of the simplistic theories of Harold Stearns and that Burke was wrong: "America is just as God-damned good as Europe—worse in some ways, better in others." And in several letters in late January he argued that, in fact, Edmund Wilson had made New York's *Vanity Fair* magazine one of the few outlets anywhere for incisive critical essays and reviews of literature, a magazine, in short, that offered opportunity for American writers to stay at home and still do good work.[48]

It was Cowley's defensiveness about American cultural promise that led him into a misunderstanding of one aspect of Dadaism, that is, the French Dadaists' ironic praise of American industrial civilization. Cowley was spending more of his days in Paris with his new Dadaist friends. Since his visits were always short, his understanding of Dadaism was mostly based on brief impressions, and he did not read all the Dada manifestos and many of the Dada writings until a decade later. In a letter of February 8 he described at length both what he admired and what he disliked in contemporary French literary life. He was impressed with the dedication to art of André Breton, Tristan Tzara, Francis Picabia, and Louis Aragon and with their sense of artistic community, a feeling Parisian artists seemed to have naturally, whereas American artists felt isolated in America. But Cowley was also impressed by, and spent considerable time with, "the hated enemies of the Dadas," his friends André Salmon and Pierre MacOrlan. Cowley found all these men extremely interesting, though he still could not accept the Dada literary doctrines he described as "the

---

idea, in "Correspondence," *Secession*, IV (January, 1923), 29–30. Cowley to Burke, January 10, 1923, n.d., 1923 file.

48. Cowley to Burke, January 28, 1923, n.d., 1923 file.

abolition of logic and communicability in art" and its aesthetic of antinaturalism.[49]

Cowley's writings in February continued his description of his ambiguous reaction to the Dadaists. In describing to Kenneth Burke the camaraderie of the Dadaist community of Paris, and their bohemian sexual behavior as well as their preference for the city, he expressed his own inability to live in cities for long periods of time: "Paris is too intense, too active. It is a town where one spends weekends which occasionally last a lifetime."[50]

Several poems published in February expressed his feeling. In one of them his desire to escape the city was the subject:

We will make our way out of the city. Come!

    It is too late now.

I know a place where blue grass, orchard grass,
red clover, timothy and white clover
are tangled in an orchard, and juneberries
ripen and fall at the deep edge of the woods.

    Crowds, turbines, unremembered time:
    it is too late now.

Since unremembered time the ferns have grown
knee-deep, and moss under the chestnut trees
hiding the footprints of small deer. We ran,
do you remember, trampling ferns to reach
a spring that issued from the chestnut roots
in a bright stream, then traced it through
               the laurel,
crossing burned ground where briars held us back
with their skinny hands, and crashing down a hill
headlong to find—

It is too late now, too late:
we have lived a great while here and no moons rise.
The juneberries will be withered on the branches,
the chestnut trees are dead.[51]

49. *Ibid.*, February 8, 1923.
50. *Ibid.*
51. Malcolm Cowley, "Poem for Two Voices," *Poetry*, XXI (February, 1923),

Another poem, which Cowley dedicated to his friend William Slater Brown of New York, echoed his pastoral theme:

With rain-washed gulleys marking where the streets
ran riverward in other days; with mounds
of marble, brick and concrete split across them,
and crazy girders bridging them, to rust
in the northeast gales;

with towers crumbling in the sunshine, lakes
of peace in every cellar, brambles hiding
the public squares, and underfoot a rat
crossing the stone jungle (the horizon
vast and empty of smoke):

no, in our lifetime we could never make
out of Manhattan Island ten good farms,
or five, or two . . . and yet the open graveyards,
the rich plots where slaughterhouses flourished
and one day fell—our gardens will be there.[52]

In three other poems published in February Cowley continued to express a conflict between his more or less professional goal of becoming a man of letters and his perhaps instinctual desire to get back to the farm. The titles and subjects of two poems in particular revealed tension. One called "Mortuary" was filled with imagery of death, while another, called "Interment," explicitly expressed a theme of urban claustrophobia:

We have lived too long together in this room,
too long in windless exile from the meadows;
boredom tonight is lurking in the shadows;
he spies on us from the gloom.[53]

In his one major article published in February Cowley articulated a theory of the proper role for writers in the modern environment. The piece, the second of his *Bookman* portraits of Paris

233–34; rpr. as "The Chestnut Trees Are Dead" in *Blue Juniata*, 30.

52. Malcolm Cowley, "Prophetic," *Poetry*, XXI (February, 1923), 237; rpr. as "Ten Good Farms (To W.S.B.)" in *Blue Juniata*, 90.

53. Malcolm Cowley, "Mortuary," *Broom*, IV (February, 1923), 170; rpr. as

literary figures, sharply attacked avant-garde withdrawal from public events. "André Salmon and His Generation," describing the man who had deeply impressed Cowley the previous summer and in his recent meetings, recounted the history of Salmon's arrival in Paris and his collaboration and friendship, around 1905, with six young artists who were destined to have enormous influence on modern French literature and art. The group of Derain, Picasso, Max Jacob, Apollinaire, Pierre MacOrlan, and Salmon was united less by a common ideology or point of view, Cowley wrote, than by common experience. Cowley here was developing a theory of "literary generations" that was to inform *Exile's Return*:

Here in America the word "generation" is apt to be misunderstood; this in spite of all the recent discussion. A literary generation is not a coterie or a society for mutual admiration. It is a group of men whose common age has given them a common point of view, and a common aim which is not necessarily the destruction of every other generation.

American writers are more apt to be influenced by their financial circumstances than by their age, but even here generations are not un-known. For example, there is the generation of hopeful intellectuals who found expression in the *New Republic*, followed by the discouraged intellectuals who write for *The Freeman*. There was the generation of psychoanalysts—the Stieglitz crowd—who founded *Seven Arts*, and latterly there has been the critical generation of *Secession*. . . . In France, where society is more closely knit, generations are an older phenome-non, defined more clearly.[54]

Cowley was partly echoing ideas derived from Salmon, but the ideas were also his own. In his theory artistic attitudes and ar-tistic work reflected the spirit of particular circumstances, one aspect of which was the impact of individuals on each other. Cowley closed his essay with another attack on the avant-garde concept of the artist as dandy, which Baudelaire and later Sym-

---

"Death" in *Blue Juniata*, 94; quotation from Cowley, "Interment," *Poetry*, XXI (February, 1923), 235–36; rpr. in *Blue Juniata*, 45.

54. Malcolm Cowley, "André Salmon and His Generation," *Bookman*, LVI (February, 1923), 714–17.

bolist artists had particularly espoused. Salmon and his friends had come to Paris as poor young men, Cowley wrote, and could not afford the insouciance and antibourgeois alienation of the earlier Symbolists. His group had reversed the stereotype of the artist as bohemian: "From their attic windows they scoffed at the aesthetic parade of the nineties. And it is largely because of this scoffing that nobody dares to live the arty life today—no artist, I mean. The poets and artists of today are practical people whose clothes are made by the best tailor they can afford and whose economic knowledge shames mere business men." Salmon's writing in particular, Cowley argued, was not limited to esoteric, private, or obscure symbols, but represented a return to an older tradition of European art: "Salmon is not essentially a critic. He is not a novelist, a reporter, not even a writer of verse. He is a type unfortunately rare in modern times: a man of letters who has taken all literature for his province, but what he means, perhaps, is very much the same."[55]

Apparently Salmon symbolized for Cowley his own developing ideal, a writer who took everything of interest to humanity as his subject and who wrote for widely read Paris newspapers on everything from murder trials to current art. Cowley ended his portrait with a quotation from Salmon that demonstrably expressed his own belief: "Art must be given back to life."[56]

Cowley's activities in January and February, 1923, had been fruitful. March was a busy month, too, filled with meeting people, writing seven book reviews, and publishing in *Broom* another imaginary portrait, this one a satire on the new American advertising symbols, particularly the all-American male, white,

55. *Ibid.*

56. *Ibid.* Salmon was apparently spitefully misrepresented in Gertrude Stein's description of the famous banquet for the "primitive" painter Henri Rousseau, the man Picasso, Derain, Braque, and others "discovered" as a model for their complete break with nineteenth-century realistic painting (*Autobiography of Alice B. Toklas*, 96–101; on page 54 Stein admitted she disliked Salmon. Salmon's own version of events was explained in his memoirs years later, never translated into English, *Souvenirs sans fin* [1955–56]).

Anglo-Saxon, blond model in a business suit. Cowley dedicated his parody of the new "marketing image" to Sinclair Lewis and his *Babbitt*, satirizing the artist J. C. Leyendecker's drawings of male models as they appeared in advertising pages during the early 1920s.[57]

Early in March, 1923, Cowley lunched in Paris with Gilbert Seldes, managing editor of the *Dial*, who was vacationing in Europe for reasons of health. Seldes told him that Kenneth Burke had been made a permanent member of the staff. While in the city Cowley also met John Peale Bishop, who informed him that Cowley's high school classmate, the actress Mary Blair, had married Edmund Wilson in New York and that Wilson had recently resigned as literary editor of *Vanity Fair*. The news from New York heightened Cowley's desire to return. Burke had located some property in northern New Jersey that could be bought for a low price. It was close to New York and yet still surrounded by countryside. Cowley was enthusiastic about joining him: "How many acres? Are there trout in the trout stream you mention? Does the garden look promising?" By this time his consuming desire was to find a permanent place to settle after years of vagrant life from Boston to New York to France.[58]

Since January the editors of *Secession*, Josephson, Munson, and now Burke, had been unable to put an issue together because of editorial quarreling, and the magazine was giving a rattle of death. Over the next year there would be only three more slim issues. Cowley, who had stayed on the sidelines of the Dada feuding as much as possible, nevertheless regretted the acrimony between his friends: "I regret this quarrel of theirs, which Munson did not seek and which was partly forced on Matty by circumstances. . . . If you are cowardly and wise you will steer away from the quarrel. I shall urge Matty to forget it, but good counsels are never heeded."[59]

57. Cowley to Burke, March 11, 1923; Cowley, "Portrait by Leyendecker," *Broom*, IV (March, 1923), 240–47.

58. Cowley to Burke, March 1, 1923.

59. *Ibid.*, March 8, 1923.

The American literary camp was folding its tents all around him in March. Harold Loeb was en route to Paris from Berlin, where he had temporarily ceased publication of *Broom* because of financial difficulties. Cowley was saddened by this turn of events, even though he had been at odds with the content of *Broom*. A phase of the American expatriate movement of the 1920s was coming to an end.

By March 17, 1923, Cowley was back in Giverny from a recent Paris visit with Tristan Tzara, Louis Aragon, John Dos Passos, and John Peale Bishop. Bishop fascinated him: "He has more information about literature than anyone else I have met." As the new editor of *Vanity Fair*, Bishop also had power to influence the public. During his Paris visit Cowley had read the March *Dial* with his Proust essay at Sylvia Beach's bookshop, and its hostility to Proust caused him doubts. But he differed with Kenneth Burke's assessment of his views: "It was . . . pompous, full of fine writing. . . . But I don't admit the charge that it was too informative. Take knowledge for granted . . . whose? . . . I must be one of ten Americans, or perhaps five, who have read the collected works of Proust." [60] Indeed, he probably was one of few who had read Proust in the original French, and his reading put him far ahead of the American public in understanding modern art.

His reaction to Burke's theories of art also led him in late March to formulate a philosophy of book reviewing, which Cowley thought was badly enough practiced in American papers to justify the ridicule turned on it by many writers:

You believe that a critic should judge a book according to aesthetic laws which he formulates. In effect, you believe in using a book as a text for an essay on Form. . . . More modest, I believe in defining a book. I believe there is no distinction, except of degree, between a book-criticism and a book-review, and that your essays in aesthetics parade under a false name. They are good essays but bad reviews.

Book reviewing is a distinctly minor medium, [although] for material reasons it has attracted a number of the best intelligences in America. Following their instincts they are attempting to elevate book-

60. *Ibid.*, March 17, 1923.

reviewing. They are succeeding, not in elevating reviews, but in writing essays. Which perhaps would be more successful if they marched under their own colors.[61]

In a letter Cowley received on March 18, 1923, Burke suggested that Cowley read Benedetto Croce's *Esthetic* (1902), presumably because of its argument that art is the expression of individual intuitions, not of social or historical circumstances. Croce, whose theories had an important influence on modern aesthetics, drew upon earlier philosophers from Hegel to Nietzsche to argue that there is a fundamental opposition between the mind's creation of art and its understanding of "natural" reality: "Knowledge has two forms: it is either *intuitive* knowledge or *logical* knowledge . . . it is the production either of images or of concepts."[62] Croce's understanding of the aesthetic sense as a subjective phenomenon and of the artist's function as one of producing images through nonlogical perceptual processes was one of many modern intellectual assaults on classical, rational aesthetics. Cowley responded to Burke's Crocean interest understandably, if we recall that his reading of Boileau had confirmed his belief in the common source of aesthetic and conceptual knowledge determined by human reason:

It happened that I was reading Croce when your letter arrived, and my disagreement with every point of his Breviary of Aesthetics is so profound that I thought of writing an Aesthetic Breviary of my own by the simple process of turning each of Croce's statements backwards. Fuck the dignity of criticism: it is the dignity of criticism which produced my essay on Proust and certain of your works which, cher ami, I shall not mention. The *honesty* of criticism: that is a more desirable quality, but not a quality to talk about, out of respect for criticism and the desire not to be a dignified ass.[63]

---

61. *Ibid.*
62. Cited in Will Durant, "Croce," *The Story of Philosophy* (1926; rpr. New York, 1961), 473.
63. Cowley to Burke, March 18, 1923.

Yet oppose the trend as he might, Cowley recognized the truth of Burke's assertion that seeing a work of art's "formal" properties as the essential measure of its value was the dominant trend of modern aesthetics. In response to this doctrine, which Cowley knew was being advocated by almost all modern art movements and theorists from Croce to Roger Fry to Russian Formalist theoreticians to the so-called Prague school of linguists, he reacted defensively but with some apparent self-doubt and irony: "Since when should subject matter undergo a priori definitions and limitation? What do you mean? . . . I'm trying to formulate my instinctive reactions to the issue. . . . I haven't swallowed Dada hook and sinker; my instincts are classical and intellectual; I'll save my soul if it can be saved. As you will save yours. . . . Abstrakten form . . . Dinamik . . . rhythmus."[64]

The third of Cowley's *Bookman* portraits of Paris writers further illustrated his dissent from modern formalist aesthetics. Published in April, it described a Paris medical doctor, Georges Duhamel, who had become a writer out of a need to communicate to a wider public his outrage at the terrible suffering caused by the world war. But the interesting quality of the essay is the manner in which Cowley again used his interview to emphasize his personal themes. He described Duhamel's style as an example of the clear writing only a highly skilled and self-confident professional can attain, as if he were a surgeon using a scalpel: "His style is remarkable for its clarity and vigor." Cowley used Duhamel's remarks to sharpen his own belief in the social function of the writer and the promise of American culture. He quoted Duhamel as saying:

The only thing that matters for a writer . . . is to know society and the individual, and to tell what he has seen. . . . Sometimes I believe, he says, that Americans mistake the meaning of civilization. Your countrymen have a tendency to treat life as a simple problem in economics, and when they do they go astray. A people defends itself with museums,

64. *Ibid.*

with libraries, with works of art, and not with banks or armies. The first question is always a moral question. . . . I love America, but not because the dollar is worth twelve francs. I love America on account of Whitman and Emerson.[65]

In early April Cowley reviewed a book of poems by Elinor Wylie for the *Dial.*[66] Though his review was not published until June, it was like his essay on Duhamel in expressing his opposition to the stylistic experimentalism of modern writing and the excessive violation of literary conventions:

Elinor Wylie writes in a medium which T. S. Eliot never attempted: magazine verse. Literature takes curious forms and magazine verse is one of them. It is bound by conventions as rigid, perhaps, as those of Racinian tragedy or the Noh drama; the perspective of a century will be needed to appreciate how they are narrow. Magazine verse must fill the bottom of a page, agreeably. It is limited to certain subjects treated with a certain degree of lyricism. . . . Apparently these conventions should prevent the writing of even passable verse, but talent thrives on conventions. Miss Wylie is talented.[67]

Much of April Cowley spent attempting to evaluate the possible future of the two little magazines which he thought his friends had done their best to destroy with their literary feuding. He reviewed material for what became the fifth issue of *Secession*, which consisted mostly of poetry, all of which was assembled by John Wheelwright, who was visiting Paris briefly and who, with Cowley's assistance, put the issue together. In early April, Josephson and Wheelwright traveled to Giverny for consultations, and Cowley later wrote that much of the competition between his young writer friends was sharpened partly by the influence of the Dadaists, who made a profession of personal feuding. In Giverny

65. Malcolm Cowley, "Duhamel, M.D.," *Bookman*, LVII (April, 1923), 160–62.

66. Cowley to Burke, April 5, 1923.

67. Malcolm Cowley, "The Owl and the Nightingale," *Dial*, LXXIV (June, 1923), 624–26.

Cowley's distance from the Paris literary feuds permitted him to admire Josephson's "charm and vitality," and Munson's obvious intelligence and "lively" writing.[68]

The writers of the Lost Generation were to be influenced for at least another year, and some of them all of their careers, by the ideas and fervor of the modernist movement in art. In late April Cowley indicated his strongest reaction to a central doctrine of that movement derived from French nineteenth-century artists: the doctrine that art is a form of salvation from the dullness of human life. He wrote Burke, "Once you wrote me in about these words. 'Any man who devotes his whole life to literature or any man who devotes his whole life to letters is a moron.' I think you were write [*sic*], and should be willing to apply the term to Flaubert with restrictions."[69]

At the end of April Cowley returned to Giverny, where the Dadaist Louis Aragon came to finish a novel. He and Cowley went walking together almost every afternoon. Aragon was a brilliant talker and, during Cowley's last months in France, became a powerful influence on him. In May and June, in a jovial and spirited concession to that friendship, Cowley participated in some Dada escapades in Paris. But his private conviction about the interrelationship of artists, society, and history was never really affected by Dadaism. In early May, for example, he took exception to Kenneth Burke's assertion that literature could be judged formally without reference to its historical background: "A house is not independent of its environment; neither is a book. As soon as one allows a book to be judged against its background instead of as a phenomenon existing in an imagined vacuum;—at that moment one allows the whole mechanics of representationalism to creep in, which is the logical defect of my position. . . . We must avoid the antithesis of form-matter; as long as we cling to it there is no way out."[70]

68. Cowley to Burke, April 5, 6, 1923.
69. *Ibid.*, April 28, 1923.
70. *Ibid.*, May 4, 1923.

His fourth *Bookman* portrait, of the poet Charles Vildrac, discussed the relationship of the modern writer to his public. It described Vildrac as a writer of integrity, who was not alienated from his audience but who at the same time upheld high literary standards and did not debase his work for the sake of giving it popular appeal. With admiration, Cowley described Vildrac as a man who wrote with honesty about what he believed. A writer of small output marked by a clear style, Vildrac seemed to reflect Cowley's own ideal, the integration of art and life.[71]

Two poems published in the May issue of the *Dial* were lyrics celebrating natural beauty:

From the bulk of it,
from summer fields pegged flat beneath the sky,
from enormous sunlight beating down on them,
I hid myself away
under the water, under green water,
where silver fishes nibbled at my thighs,
                    saying:

"We swam upstream for three days and three nights;
we drifted three days southward with the current,
and nowhere found a limit to the world.
It is shaped like a willow branch. No one can swim
                    to the tip."
The fishes hid away beneath a stone.

The second poem was an impression of dusk at Giverny:

Starlings wheel and descend at nightfall, choosing
        maybe a bamboo copse or a cedar of Lebanon.
        They cross the face of the winter sun like a smoke.

A cloud of descending starlings: it takes the shape
        successively of a ball, a cane, a mandolin—
        or rather a guitar—a string of frankfurters,

71. Malcolm Cowley, "Charles Vildrac," *Bookman*, LVII (May, 1923), 291–94.

a candy-poke, finally a balloon that collapses
with a rush of escaping gases;

out of the center of a cloud is heard the twitter-
ing of birds.[72]

By the end of May Cowley was making plans to return to New York during the first week of August. He arranged his sailing plans, and he obtained the rights to translate the works of some Paris friends such as Salmon and Pierre MacOrlan, then a best-selling French author. He intended to settle near New York and attempt to earn a living as a free-lance writer. On May 20 he reported to Burke on luncheon meetings with Gilbert Seldes and e. e. cummings. Seldes cleared payment to him of two hundred dollars for work Cowley had done for the *Dial*.[73] The money helped him survive during his last weeks in France. He was dead broke.

Two friends occupied Cowley's time during the last week of May. In meetings with Harold Loeb in Giverny, Cowley learned of his hope of reviving *Broom* in New York, but with its focus shifted from modern European art to the work of American writers such as Hart Crane, Jean Toomer, Glenway Westcott, and Yvor Winters and to the young poets and writers of Cowley's circle. Loeb's list of writers showed Cowley's influence and his astute awareness of the promising new writers in New York.[74]

Cowley's growing influence on his friends was evident also in an essay Kenneth Burke published in the June *Dial* comparing the poetry of John Milton and Gertrude Stein. Burke challenged the theory of "significant form" that Clive Bell was developing in various New York journals in 1923 and that he would incorporate in *Art*, a central treatise of the avant-garde aesthetic. Burke disputed Bell's assertion that the form of a work of art alone created

72. Malcolm Cowley, "The Fishes," and "The Starlings," *Dial*, LXXIV (May, 1923), 133–34 and 494.
73. Cowley to Burke, n.d., May, 1923, May 20, 1923.
74. *Ibid.*, n.d., May, 1923.

aesthetic response. He argued that the intellectual content of literature also determined the reaction of an audience: "Miss Stein's verse is the return to the primitive. But Milton's line has something more than Miss Stein's. The significant form is backed by subject matter, and this backing produces a heightened emotion. . . . Art, that is, is a process of individualization; form is general, subject matter is specific." [75]

Several of Burke's essays from the *Dial* in 1922 and 1923 were incorporated in *Counter-Statement* in 1931 and described modern literature's exclusively "aesthetic" concerns. Those essays reflected his debates with Cowley over several years about the issues of modern aesthetic formalism and the social alienation of artists. It is the only influence on Burke's speculative works that Cowley will admit to. [76]

He read and agreed with Burke's essay, but in June his high spirits perversely made him reverse his position (now that Burke was seeing things Cowley's way) and declare he was becoming a modernist:

I am going over to the damned unconscious school of writers, having discovered that my best phrases are really an inspiration. No, damnation, I am not going over to the unconscious school. I continue to abjure their Franks and Andersons. But I have found that my own unconscious is often a shortcut to better work than I can do consciously, and I am trying to make the best use of this unexpected tool. Consciously. [77]

In a long description of Louis Aragon, Cowley told about the fervor of Aragon's "moral" criterion for judging writers. He confessed that Aragon's Dadaist enthusiasm had partly infected him in recent weeks, whimsically inspiring him to "reform the world" through art. Cowley quoted this letter in *Exile's Return*, when he

75. Kenneth Burke, "Engineering with Words," *Dial*, LXXIV (June, 1923), 408–12.

76. Interview with Malcolm Cowley by author, July, 1975.

77. Cowley to Burke, June 4, 1923.

satirized his own brief, exuberant participation in Dada in the late spring of 1923.[78]

But as his record shows, Cowley had encountered the social, aesthetic, and cultural ideas of modern art in Europe during the 1920s only to reject them. A major essay on the drama of Jean Racine, on which Cowley spent almost the entire month of June, summarized his literary beliefs acquired from a two-year journey to the center of the European avant-garde. In a letter written in early June he indicated that he saw Racine as a writer integrated into his society and supported by it, a status he saw as his own ideal. He mentioned that he had earned $654 by his writing during the past year, and this small success encouraged him to hope that he could earn a living in America as a professional writer. Cowley dreamed of writing like Racine about everything concerning society in his time: "We are poets—not critics, and are therefore interested in all human activity. I do not want to be categorized in a narrow role."[79]

His month's work evaluating Racine and the French classical theater produced a long essay which he had privately printed in two hundred copies. The essay stated the beliefs about art and literature that he had developed over more than two years of reaction to modern art and aesthetic theory. It thus represented his most considered statement of his own literary values:

My essay is not on the beauty of Racine's diction but on the conventions of his theatre, suggesting that the existence of conventions is more important than their exact nature. I end with a discussion of the need of a historical definition of classicism, to place beside the historical definition of romanticism, suggest Racine as the classical type par excellence, and in a tangent point out that the whole classical movement is only a part of literature and not the ideal for everybody.[80]

78. *Ibid.*; Malcolm Cowley, *Exile's Return: A Literary Odyssey of the Nineteen Twenties* (New York, 1951), 163.

79. Cowley to Burke, July 5, June 9, 29, 1923.

80. *Ibid.*, June 16, 1923.

Racine's stylish clarity and his interest in social behavior contrasted with what Cowley believed was the pettiness of a good deal of avant-garde art. In a letter to Burke he described the latter as lacking in social concern: "We must use one issue of *Broom* to satirize the hypocrisy of American laws like Prohibition otherwise we will resign ourselves to petty literary wars with Ezra Pound, Robert McAlmon, and Floyd Dell."[81]

Although he still could not define his philosophy of life before leaving France in August, he knew that the experience had been formative. The Racine essay, which Cowley also sent to Van Wyck Brooks for publication in the *Freeman*, expressed his belief that literature should treat as subject matter issues of human concern and should use traditional artistic conventions to communicate with the public:

Versailles is one of two perfect expressions of the seventeenth century in France. The other is the tragedies of Jean Racine.

He expressed a definite society and therefore could not exist without it. . . . If all these means of vulgarizing literature are justified it is only to form an intelligent public, which in turn exists to make an intelligent literature possible. . . . The seventeenth century produced Racine as a sort of natural fruit. . . . What it produced was a milieu in which he could exist as a dramatist. . . . The elements of literature are not words but emotions and ideas. To be abstract a literature need not be unintelligible; on the contrary. An abstract literature is one in which ideas or emotions, expressed with the greatest possible exactness, are combined into a unity which possesses a formal value, and which is something more than a copy of experience. Evidently Racine comes nearer this ideal than Gertrude Stein and immensely nearer than our contemporary neo-classicists, most of whom have never even conceived it. The Racinians of to-day are not writers but painters; men like Picasso or Braque whose attitude toward the exterior world is much the same as his, and who, by utilizing conventions almost in his fashion, arrive at a fantastically similar result. They invent most of their own conventions; Racine was more fortunately born to observe those which existed al-

81. *Ibid.*, June 29, 1923.

ready. He demanded a discipline. Left to himself he would have evolved another set of rules, but he would have followed them as faithfully and it is doubtful whether they would have served his purpose better . . . for it is only by the existence of such concrete traditions and an audience trained in them that the classical theatre becomes possible . . . It is difficult to analyse the impression that persists after a tragedy by Racine, especially because it has always been outside my powers to decide whether a given emotion was moral or aesthetic. I admire the facility with which the disciples of Croce settle such questions, but in the case of Racine aesthetics and morality are mingled to such a degree that it requires nothing less than a Crocean act of faith to disentangle them. Racine himself made no such attempt. . . . Can a pure aesthetic exist? To deny that literature has moral significance leaves the conception of morality intact but it subtracts an important element from literature. . . . As a matter of fact, the Racinian tragedy, for all its plastic value, is moral to a supreme degree. It is moral for reasons which neither Croce nor Racine himself has mentioned: because it reasserts, in the face of doubts which assail us constantly, the importance of man's destiny, the reality of his passions, the dignity of the human animal.[82]

In 1955 the critic Wylie Sypher described the essay as the best ever written on Racine in English, and he used it to support his thesis that the evolution of Renaissance art, from rational objective perspective through periods of excessive emotional stylistic distortion and finally to a neoclassical "discipline of emotion by reason," was symbolized by Racine's style, which Cowley had so acutely defined.[83]

In searching for a way to define a functional relationship between literature and human life, Cowley had returned to older doctrines of classical humanism. Literature was a mirror of life, having as its purpose the education of men in the knowledge of human personality and values. The essay concluded with Cowley's definition of what he believed constituted a classical literature,

82. Malcolm Cowley, "Racine," *Freeman*, October 10, 1923, pp. 104–106; and October 17, 1923, 132–33.
83. Wylie Sypher, *Four Stages of Renaissance Style* (New York, 1955), 297.

which he held as his own ideal in contrast to what he believed was the continuing Romanticism of modern art.

My ideal of classicism is an approach, through arbitrary conventions, to a form which is perfect and abstract. It remains intelligible at the same time, and human. It is concerned with people instead of with nature or the supernatural; it considers the moral rather than the picturesque value of their action; it does not avoid their most rigorous ideas or their most violent emotions . . . it is not the only ideal. As long as a nation retains its vitality, classical and romantic periods succeed each other. The desire for change is the most durable convention. Unquestionably the last age was romantic.[84]

In early August, 1923, Cowley sailed back to New York.

84. Cowley, "Racine," 132–33.

CHAPTER 6

One Exile's Return

When the Cowleys landed at the French Line pier early in August, 1923, he had only five dollars in his pocket, with a little loose silver and nickels to feed the telephone. He did not even know where to dispatch their big wicker trunk. A series of telephone calls solved their immediate problems. A friend of Peggy's had taken a little house far downtown, almost in the shadow of the Woolworth Building. The trunk could go there and the Cowleys, too, because the rubbish-cluttered top floor of the house was for rent. But first they took a taxi to the big room in the Village, near Fifth Avenue, where Matthew and Hannah Josephson were then living in modest comfort.

Josephson had revived *Broom* in New York, after finding a printer moderately interested in rebel art and willing to extend him credit, at least for a time. He at once invited Cowley to be his associate editor, without salary of course. The problem of livelihood remained for Cowley, but it was solved after a fashion on the following day. He paid a visit to *Sweet's Architectural Catalogue*, from which he had resigned before leaving for France, and found that the editor was desperately trying to bring out a new annual edition on schedule. Cowley was hired back and was asked to start work immediately.

He has told the disastrous but in many ways farcical story of his return to New York in Chapter VI of *Exile's Return*. He tried to do too much. During the first two months he was working under pressure at *Sweet's* for nine or ten hours a day. At the same time he was helping Josephson keep their magazine alive, and this involved reading manuscripts and getting them ready for the printer, besides searching for talented contributors. As an ultimate goal, they were trying to re-create, in New York, the literary atmosphere of youth and lively defiance that had so impressed them in Paris.

It is to be said again that Cowley had been attracted to what might be called the literary ethics of Dadaism, that is, its high sense of personal integrity and its sometimes violent rejection of the conventional wisdom that prevailed among older writers. Cowley liked the feeling that he belonged to a rebellious league of youth. On the other hand, he remained dubious about the aesthetic doctrines proclaimed by his French friends and more than dubious about their celebration of the unconscious and the irrational. He did accept for a time—if more hesitantly than Josephson—one favorite theme of the rebel writers, namely, their admiration of the machine age, its skyscrapers, and its advertising slogans. Still, he never became a Skyscraper Primitive, in a phrase of the time. His heart remained in the countryside.

After the huge nineteenth edition of *Sweet's Architectural Catalogue* went to press in October, Cowley had a little more time for undertakings in the literary world. Not one of these was successful. Soon it became evident that the dream he shared with Josephson of re-creating Paris in New York was leading to a series of disasters. The first of these was a meeting they assembled in an Italian restaurant to mobilize support for *Broom* and perhaps for wider activities. There were too many personal grudges among those invited, and the meeting dissolved into noisy altercations. Two or three weeks later came a financial blow. *Broom's* obliging printer rebelled against its unpaid debts and refused to set the December issue in type. Josephson found a cheaper printer, but one who demanded to be paid in cash. The weather was turning cold. For some weeks Cowley scurried about raising money from reluctant donors at a cost to himself of time and pride.

In December, 1923, after *Broom's* new printer had been paid in advance, the first number of the *American Mercury* appeared on the newsstands in its green cover. One feature of the number was an imaginary portrait by Ernest Boyd, the Irish critic, called "Aes-

thete: Model 1924." Cowley, whose nerves were on edge, interpreted the portrait as a slanderous attack on his group of friends.
He retorted by abusing Boyd in the best Dada manner. The abuse
was purely verbal, but Boyd thought he was being threatened
with physical violence. The episode was embroidered in literary
columns and further embroidered in gossip. Many people felt
that Cowley had made a fool of himself, and this time Cowley was
not sure that they were wrong.

Then came a final blow to his ambitions. The latest issue of
Broom, dated January, 1924, was ready for distribution to sub-
scribers and bookstores. It might have brought in a little money
to pay for later issues. But on January 14, the editors received a
notice from the postmaster general: the issue had been suppressed
under Section 480 of the postal laws, which prohibited the mail-
ing of contraceptives and other obscene matter. Actually, the
issue was not in the least obscene; it was not even mildly sala-
cious. The suppression, apparently based on the prejudice against
little magazines of a single postal inspector, might well have been
overruled in a federal court if the editors had been able to bring
suit. But they had no money to hire a lawyer, let alone print future issues. Effectively the publication of *Broom* had ended.

Cowley tried to lay new plans, but he was too exhausted and
discouraged to carry them out. Late on an icy February night, he
wrote a brief letter to himself:

My dear Malcolm [the letter read in part], it would be wise to admit
that you were mistaken and that you cannot, while working for Sweet's
Catalogue Service, Inc., be editor, free lance, boon companion, literary
polemist. Instead you must confine yourself to essentials: thinking,
reading, conversation, livelihood, in about the order named. At this
moment you must strip yourself of everything inessential to these aims;
and especially of the functions of editor, free lance, drinking companion
and literary polemist. . . . You have left the stage and you did not
even bow.[1]

1. This account of Cowley's early months in New York is mostly summarized
from chapter IV of *Exile's Return: A Literary Odyssey of the Nineteen Twenties* (New
York, 1951). Cowley's letter to himself appears on page 201.

During that period of discouragement, Cowley was less than usually productive. He published only six book reviews in 1924, though he wrote some poems, none of which would be printed until much later.[2] One 1924 poem was "The Urn," an unrhymed sonnet that expressed his deep attachment to the countryside of his boyhood:

Wanderers outside the gate, in hollow
landscapes without memory, we carry
each of us an urn of native soil,
of not impalpable dust a double handful,

why kept, how gathered?—was it garden mould
or wood soil fresh with hemlock needles, pine,
and princess pine, this little earth we bore
in secret, blindly, over the frontier?

—a parcel of the soil not wide enough
or firm enough to build a dwelling on
or deep enough to dig a grave, but cool
and sweet enough to sink the nostrils in
and find the smell of home, or in the ears
rumors of home like oceans in a shell.[3]

Cowley was speaking for his uprooted generation, as he would later speak in *Exile's Return*. "The Urn" and other lyrics reveal his sensitivity to the elegiac themes and images of a vanishing nineteenth-century America, which were also mirrored in the turbulent fiction of the great writers of his generation such as Hemingway, Faulkner, Wolfe, and Fitzgerald.

As the months passed, Cowley emerged from his period of dejection. He began to outline a more modest but realistic and possibly fruitful program for life as an independent writer on the

2. Diane U. Eisenberg, *Malcolm Cowley: A Checklist of His Writings, 1916–1973* (Carbondale, 1975), gives a year-by-year list of his published writings. The yearly listings grow longer after 1924.

3. "The Urn" was first printed in *Poetry*, XXIX (November, 1926), 70. It was revised over the years without being radically changed. The version here reprinted is from *Blue Juniata: Collected Poems* (New York, 1968), 142.

margin of a business culture. For a time he continued to be a copywriter at *Sweet's Catalogue*; it was honest nine-to-five work if it had no literary value. Meanwhile, he published miscellaneous pieces in a variety of periodicals so as to have an unsalaried source of income. Doggedly he prepared to live in the country as a free-lance writer.

That program was carried out in modest stages. First, he moved to Staten Island, where he acquired a stock of garden tools and an ancient Ford. Second, after a year he resigned from *Sweet's* and tried the experiment of living on what he wrote. The Cowleys did not live well, even with a garden, but neither did they starve. Friends with similar tastes found them a farmhouse that rented for ten dollars a month. By then it was the spring of 1926, and the Cowleys were ready for the third and final step of his program to become a self-supporting free-lance writer. They loaded their belongings on a rickety truck, hired for the occasion, and rattled their way to Sherman, Connecticut, seventy miles north of Manhattan.[4]

Cowley's early years were a struggle, but one is impressed by how much writing he produced during the late 1920s. The writing provides a record of extraordinary energy and a constant effort to express opinions that were close to his heart. He wrote for a variety of periodicals, each of them intended for a different body of readers. Some of these magazines were unsophisticated, but Cowley did not write down to them or sugar-glaze his opinions for New Jersey housewives. One of his aims was to help in creating a general cultivated audience such as was addressed by authors of the eighteenth-century Enlightenment. Cowley was fortunate in his relations with the monthly *Dial* and with the editor of the New York *Herald Tribune* weekly literary supplement, *Books*. The first of these published several of his more thoughtful essays. The new editor of the *Herald Tribune Books*, Irita Van Doren, more or less adopted him after 1925 and rou-

4. Cowley's step-by-step program for moving to the country is detailed in an unpublished manuscript sent to the author July 11, 1983.

tinely assigned him for review almost all books by leading French authors. Thus he had opportunities to amplify his observations on the techniques of modernism and on its choice of subject matter.

One such opportunity was his front-page review of André Gide's impressive novel *The Counterfeiters* in the September 25, 1927, issue. Cowley discussed the tendency of modern fiction to adopt radically experimental forms of narration. Gide had adopted them, too, Cowley said, while exploring as radical a subject matter as any avant-garde novelist. But Cowley pointed out that Gide's novel also revitalized the great tradition of the European novel, for it demonstrated lucid exposition and narration. It remained not only extremely intelligent but also intelligible to a general audience.

Cowley wrote other reviews on similar broad themes. During the same years he translated eight books from the French. Some of these reached a fairly popular audience (Joseph Delteil's *Joan of Arc,* 1926, and Princess Bibesco's *Catherine-Paris,* 1928), and others, such as Raymond Radiguet's *The Count's Ball* (1929), became minor classics of modern literature. The most brilliant of his translations was that of Paul Valéry's first volume of essays, *Variety,* on which he worked during the summer and fall of 1926. When the book appeared early the following year, it was with an introduction that Cowley had printed in the *New Republic* at the invitation of Edmund Wilson. Part of that introduction forcefully restated Cowley's belief in liberal humanism:

From the two introductory letters . . . to the profound analysis of Leonardo da Vinci . . . everything [in Valéry's book] is directed toward a defense of the intellect, of the conscious mind. It has need of defenders in our time. Against Freudianism, for example; not in its legitimate applications, but in its literary aspects, where it results in the notion that poems are comparable in every respect with dreams. Against the super-realists. Against that school of writers led by Anderson and Lawrence which counsels drift and surrender to our instincts. Against the metaphysics of behaviorism. Against the sociological theory of art— that it is determined entirely by social and economic factors: add x to y

and Shakespeare is the result. Against determinisms in general. Against Spengler's idea that, ours being a declining civilization, we have nothing left but to sail ships and make ourselves millionaires. . . .

But among all the enemies of conscious thought, it is specialization which is the most paralyzing. It results in the idea that a real gulf exists between the different activities of the mind: as, for example, between the arts and the sciences. By confining even the great talents to one side or another of the gulf, it limits progress in both fields of endeavor. Moreover, specialization, any specialization, becomes a fixed idea, which is a form of hypnosis.[5]

Cowley was arguing that, instead of submitting to the chaos of feelings and ideas seemingly imposed on us by the modern age, writers should clarify their own values; that they should become generalists, not specialists; that they should work within society to create order, not further to isolate and fragment the arts. Unfortunately, the essay was forgotten by later audiences, but part of its message was transmitted to them by an indirect means. Edmund Wilson had read it with attention before accepting it for the *New Republic.* The closing pages of his *Axel's Castle* largely echo Cowley's plea for the defense of the intellect as the best hope for modern man.

By 1928 Cowley was beginning to express his feeling that writers—and others as well—would profit by having stronger bonds with a community. A letter to Kenneth Burke written August 18, 1928, acknowledged the influence on his thinking of a never-translated novel by Maurice Barrès, *Les Déracinés* (The uprooted). The spiritual isolation felt by many modern artists was partly the result, he argued, of their lack of integration into a society that would accept their work on its own terms. In an article of the same period, "My Countryside, Then and Now" (*Harper's,* January, 1929), Cowley told of revisiting the village where he was born. The countryside had been ravaged by industry, the woods chopped down, the streams poisoned with sulphur

5. In *New Republic*, December 8, 1926, pp. 69–71, the introduction was titled "Toward a Universal Mind."

from the mines, but human resources remained and the community was revitalizing itself. There was a lesson here—though Cowley left it implicit—for other American communities.

Already his published work was reflecting a broader interest in social and economic issues, particularly as these affected the art and profession of writing. He was urging writers to take a stand on such issues, and not only for the betterment of American culture. He also thought that it was psychologically healthy for them to accept moral and social responsibility.

In the summer and fall of 1929, he wrote a number of literary essays for his friendly editor, Irita Van Doren. The first two of these, published in June, dealt with the problems faced by his own generation of writers and with the trap (as he regarded it) of scientific pessimism; those two themes were interlinked in his mind. As an example of scientific pessimism he chose Joseph Wood Krutch, whose book *The Modern Temper* he took as an American analogue of Oswald Spengler's vast work, *The Decline of the West.* The answer to their bleak picture, he said, was the evidence provided by modern life itself and by the brilliant work of modern writers, who in various ways had tried to find values amid the chaos of the age. Each generation, he said, must rediscover "the sense of tremendous possibilities" offered by life on this earth.[6]

Four other essays appeared in New York *Herald Tribune Books* during October and November. One of them, "Machine-Made America," discussed various attacks (there was a spate of such books at the time) on what their authors presented as "this ugly civilization," wholly devoted to mass production and consumption. While admitting that there was substance in the charges, Cowley asked:

Why after all must we escape from American life? . . . We can resist mass consumption society by choice without leaving our personal com-

6. Those first two essays were "Our Own Generation," New York *Herald Tribune Books*, June 23, 1929, pp. 1, 6; and "The New Primitives," *ibid.*, June 30, 1929, pp. 1, 6.

munities and still achieve individual freedom and artistic success. . . .
The present generation in American letters offers a certain negative
proof of this assertion. It is by no means a lost generation, but it is
certainly uprooted . . . its members have paid a heavy penalty for de-
serting their own backgrounds. They are forced to write about indefinite subjects for an indefinite audience.[7]

Another of the essays for *Books* was called "The Escape from
America." One subject discussed in it was the ideas of Pound and
Eliot, whose alienation from modern society had deeply affected
other artists. Their answer to the plight of the contemporary
world was what Cowley called an impossible dream of escape into
the past. To find refuge from "the vast standardization of American life, the noise, filth and overcrowding of cities," they nour-
ished the dream "of retreat to an island or . . . the shores of an
old continent . . . where artists and philosophers are honored
among men." Cowley urged that artists and intellectuals should
abandon that fashionable dream and begin to recognize once more
the beauty of the natural and social world.[8]

Many of the ideas advanced in that series of essays for *Herald
Tribune Books* would reappear in *Exile's Return*, where they were
revised and amplified and also given a narrative framework. The
series as a whole was in some respects a first draft of *Exile's Return*.

A final essay in the series, "The Business of Being a Poet," appeared November 17, less than a month after Black Thursday on
Wall Street. It was not a timely essay because its subject was the
financial plight of poets in an American world that still seemed
prosperous. Poets were undergoing hardships long before others
did. That November was a time when nobody foresaw the later
sequel to the Wall Street crash or realized that a prolonged depression, not renewed prosperity, was "just around the corner."

In early October—that is, before the crash—Cowley had
joined the staff of the *New Republic*. He began working there

7. Malcolm Cowley, "Machine-Made America," New York *Herald Tribune
Books*, November 3, 1929, pp. 1, 6.
8. Malcolm Cowley, "The Escape from America," New York *Herald Tribune
Books*, November 10, 1929, pp. 1, 6.

part of each week as an editorial assistant, but soon he was named a full editor and was placed in charge of the book department. It was a responsible position and one that forced him to change his style of life. He could no longer write at leisure in the country. For the next few years he became an unwilling New Yorker. It was not until 1929 that he was able, by piling mortgage on mortgage, to build a modest house in the country for himself and his new wife. There he still lives and works after nearly half a century.

For a dozen years after 1929, most of his writing was first printed in the *New Republic*, which then described itself as a "journal of opinion." Cowley was not an opinionated man, except in literary matters, but the crisis in American life forced him to take more stands on political and social questions. *The New Republic* was examining the causes and nature of the Depression and was offering remedies, which became more radical as the Depression deepened. Cowley, impatient with half measures, was more of a radical than his senior colleagues. For a time he regarded himself as a Marxist and allied himself with the Communists, though without surrendering his independence of judgment; thus he condemned other Marxist critics for being dogmatic and for subordinating human values to so-called revolutionary values. At the end of the decade he became as disillusioned as others with Russian policy and where it was leading. Russia had chosen the wrong road to a happier future. Cowley's instinctive but delayed response was to forsake politics completely and devote himself to the past and contemporary record of American letters.

The present study has not dealt with these later developments in his career nor has it reconsidered his many books. Rather, it has tried to present "the long foreground," as Ralph Waldo Emerson would have called it, of his work over the years. One feature of that foreground that has impressed this writer is the consistency of his feelings about literature and life. Cowley was a country boy, as he has often said, and his attachment to the countryside has never weakened. His other attachment has been to the art of letters. He lived among modernists and admired their technical brilliance as well as their defiant code of literary ethics, but he never ceased to question their aesthetic doctrines, which, he believed, might lead to disastrous consequences in daily life. He had a strong sense of community with other writers and thought of himself as belonging to an international republic of letters. There have been changes, sometimes complete, in his attitudes, but these underlying beliefs have persisted from the beginning.

In a Foreword to *And I Worked at the Writer's Trade* (1978) Cowley says:

The author has to confess that, in these later years, he has felt increasingly alone and beleaguered. He is, after all, a humanist by instinct, one who believes that literature should deal with persons (though it may also deal with animals, objects, or forces that exist as persons for the reader). He believes in the reciprocal connection between artists and their audience. He believes that literature comes out of life—where else could it come from?—and that, if successful in its own terms, it goes back into life by changing the consciousness of its readers. All these are primer-book notions, but, during the last few years, they have been less universally accepted. It seems to the author—it seems to me—that much of our fiction, much of our poetry, and a substantial body of our criticism have become more and more unpeopled, unliving, and even inhuman. But fashions will change, as they always do.[9]

In his eightieth year Cowley was expressing the sense of literary values that gave substance to his essay on Racine, published for a very small audience when he was only twenty-five years old. He was continuing his long battle against fashions in literature and against aesthetic doctrines that by now had outwardly assumed a different form but that he still regarded as harmful to writers as persons. Cowley has been true to the literary and social values he developed early in his career. Throughout his long and significant career, he remained what he was in the beginning, a humanist among the moderns.

9. Malcolm Cowley, *And I Worked at the Writer's Trade* (New York, 1978), x.

Selected Bibliography

Manuscript Collections and Periodicals

MALCOLM COWLEY PAPERS, NEWBERRY LIBRARY, CHICAGO.

This collection, some of which remains uncataloged, consists of twenty-four boxes of correspondence to Cowley dating from 1920 to 1968 and six boxes of letters written by Cowley dating from 1915 to 1968. Additional file boxes contain significant correspondence between Cowley and persons with whom he was associated at the Yaddo writers' colony from approximately 1940 to 1968 and at the National Institute of Arts and Letters. Various other file boxes contain correspondence and manuscripts relating to Cowley's writing projects and his thirty-year tenure as literary consultant to the Viking Press of New York. I did not consult Cowley's correspondence after 1968, although the Newberry acquired that correspondence in 1979.

"LITTLE" MAGAZINES AND OTHER PERIODICALS

Broom. Edited by Harold Loeb *et al.* New York, 1921–24.
Dial. New York, 1920–25.
Freeman. New York, 1920–24.
Little Review. Chicago, New York, London, 1914–29.
New Republic. New York, 1920–40.
Partisan Review. New York, 1936–39.
Secession. Edited by Gorham B. Munson *et al.* 1922–24. New York: Kraus Reprint Service, 1967.
Transatlantic Review. Edited by Ford Madox Ford. Paris, January–December 1924.

Works by Malcolm Cowley

WORKS WRITTEN BY COWLEY

After the Genteel Tradition: American Writers, 1910–1930. Carbondale, 1964.

And I Worked at the Writer's Trade. New York, 1978.

Blue Juniata. New York, 1929.

Blue Juniata: Collected Poems. New York, 1968.

The Dream of the Golden Mountains: Remembering the 1930's. New York, 1980.

The Dry Season. Norfolk, Conn., 1941.

Exile's Return: A Narrative of Ideas. New York, 1934; revised as *Exile's Return: A Literary Odyssey of the Nineteen Twenties.* New York, 1951.

The Faulkner-Cowley File: Letters and Memories, 1944–1962. New York, 1966.

The Literary Situation. New York, 1954.

A Many Windowed House: Collected Essays on American Writers and American Writing. Carbondale, 1970.

A Second Flowering: Works and Days of the Lost Generation. New York, 1974.

Think Back on Us . . . A Contemporary Chronicle of the 1930's. Edited by Henry Dan Piper. Carbondale, 1967.

WORKS EDITED BY COWLEY (GENERALLY INCLUDE INTRODUCTORY ESSAYS)

Books That Changed Our Minds. New York, 1939.

The Portable Faulkner. New York, 1946; rev. ed., 1967.

The Portable Hawthorne. New York, 1948.

The Portable Hemingway. New York, 1944.

Walt Whitman's Leaves of Grass: The First (1855) Edition. New York, 1959.

Winesburg Ohio. New York, 1960.

The Works of Walt Whitman: The Deathbed Edition in Two Volumes. New York, 1948; rpr. 1969.

Writers at Work: The Paris Review Interviews. 1st Series. New York, 1958.

With Robert Cowley: *Fitzgerald and the Jazz Age*. New York, 1966.
With Howard E. Hugo: *The Lessons of the Masters: An Anthology of the Novel from Cervantes to Hemingway*. New York, 1971.

WORKS TRANSLATED BY COWLEY

Catherine-Paris, by Princess Marthe Bibesco. New York, 1928.
The Count's Ball, by Raymond Radiguet. New York, 1929.
The Green Parrot, by Princess Marthe Bibesco. New York, 1929.
Joan of Arc, by Joseph Delteil. New York, 1926.
On Board the Morning Star, by Pierre MacOrlan. New York, 1924.
Variety, by Paul Valéry. New York, 1927.
With James R. Lawler: *Leonardo, Poe, Mallarmé*. Vol. 8 of *The Collected Works of Paul Valéry*. Princeton, 1972.
A complete bibliography of Cowley's published writings to 1973 is available from Southern Illinois University Press. See Diane U. Eisenberg, *Malcolm Cowley: A Checklist of His Writings, 1916–1973*. Carbondale, 1975.

Books and Essays That Discuss Cowley; Interviews

Aldridge, John W. *After the Lost Generation*. New York, 1958.
Alter, Robert. "The Travels of Malcolm Cowley." *Commentary*, LXX (August, 1980), 33–40.
Cheever, John. "My Friend, Malcolm Cowley." *New York Times Book Review*, August 28, 1983, pp. 7, 18.
Core, George. "Malcolm Cowley 1898–." In *American Writers: A Collection of Literary Biographies*. Edited by A. Walton Litz. Supplement II, Part I, pp. 135–56. New York, 1981.
Cowley, Robert. "Malcolm Cowley: Countryman." *Country Journal*, October 10, 1983, pp. 62–70.
Eisenberg, Diane U. "A Conversation with Malcolm Cowley." *Southern Review*, XV (Spring, 1979), 288–99.
Epstein, Joseph. "A Conspiracy of Silence." *Harper's*, CCLV (November, 1977), 77–92.
Gambaccini, Peter. "Last of the 'Lost Generation.'" *Yankee*, March 3, 1983, pp. 92, 123–30.

Kazin, Alfred. *Starting out in the Thirties*. Boston, 1965.

Kempf, James M. "Malcolm Cowley." In *A Critical Survey of Poetry*, pp. 598–609. Los Angeles, 1982.

Lasch, Christopher. *The New Radicalism in America, 1889–1963*. New York, 1965.

McCall, John, and George Plimpton. "The Art of Fiction LXX: Malcolm Cowley." *Paris Review*, LXXXV (n.d.), 52–75.

Piper, Henry Dan. Introduction to Malcolm Cowley, *Think Back on Us: A Contemporary Chronicle of the 1930's*. Carbondale, 1967.

Shi, David E. "Malcolm Cowley and Literary New York." *Virginia Quarterly Review*, LVIII (Autumn, 1982), 575–93.

Simpson, Lewis P. "Malcolm Cowley and the American Writer." *Sewanee Review*, LXXXIV (Spring, 1976), 220–47; rpr. Simpson, *The Brazen Face of History*. Baton Rouge, 1980.

Whittemore, Reed. "Books Considered." *New Republic*, April 29, 1978, pp. 29–31.

Wolff, Geoffrey. *Black Sun: The Brief Transit and Violent Eclipse of Harry Crosby*. New York, 1976.

Young, Philip. "For Malcolm Cowley: Critic, Poet, 1898–." *Southern Review*, IX (Autumn, 1973), 778–95.

Index